$ 21

STORIES OF PUNISHMENTS
LESSONS, & EXHORTATIONS

SHAYKH HAMOOD IBN ABDULLAH AL-TUWAIJRI

ISBN: 978-1-7923-7548-4

First Edition: Rajab 1443 AH / February 2022 CE

Cover Design: Aljadeed Design Co.
Website: www.Aljadeed.Design

Translator: Rasheed Barbee

Editing & Typesetting: Razan Gregory

Publisher's Information:
Authentic Statements Publishing
P. O. Box 15536
Philadelphia, PA. 19131
215.382.3382
215.382.3782-Fax

Store:
5000 Locust Street (Side Entrance)
Philadelphia, Pa 19139

Website: www.authenticstatements.com
E-mail: info@authenticstatements.com

Please visit our website for upcoming publications, audio/DVD online catalog, and info on events and seminars, insha Allāh.

TABLE OF CONTENTS

Biography of Author 1

    Birth and Lineage 1
    His Studies 1
    His Works 2
    His Students 3
    His Character 3
    His Death 4

.... 1

  Destruction of Previous Nations 1
  The Muslim Nation's Protection from Complete Eradication 4
  Punishments Upon Individuals from Previous Nations and This Nation 6
  The Man Who Dragged His Garment Out of Pride and Arrogance 7
  The Man and Woman Who Violated the Sanctity of the Sacred Ka'bah 8
  The Man Who Stole from the Ka'bah 10
  The Gang of Men Who Attempted to Rob the Ka'bah 11
  Men Who Pledged a False Oath at the Ka'bah 11
  The Man Who Belittled the Du'a at the Ka'bah 12
  The Thief Who Gave False Oath at the Station of Ibrahim 13
  Abraha, the Aksumite Army General Who Intended to Destroy the Ka'bah 14
  The Wretched Man Who Stole the Black Stone 14

Those Who Mocked the Messenger of Allah 16
The Five Chieftains Who Mocked the Messenger of Allah 16
Warning to Those Who Mock Hadith 18
Men Who Threw the Camel Afterbirth on the Prophet While He Was Praying 23
The Three Main Antagonists of the Messenger of Allah 27
The Story of Abu Jahl 28
The Story of Abu Lahab 30
The Story of 'Uqba ibn Abu Mu'ait 31
The Story of Umm Jamil, the Wife of Abu Lahab 32
The Story of 'Utbah, the Son of Abu Jahl 32
The Story of 'Ubay ibn Khalaf 34
The Story of Nawfal ibn Khuwaylid 35
The Story of Nadr ibn al-Harith 35
The Story of 'Amir ibn Tufayl and Arbad ibn Qays 36
The Roman Who Intended to Disrespect the Grave of the Prophet 39
The Arrogant Man Who Denied the Existence of Allah 40
The Man Who Ridiculed the Miswak 40
The Man Who Belied the Decree of Allah 42
Those Who Insulted Abu Bakr and 'Umar 42
The Dog and Sufyan at-Thawri 44
Those Who Insulted Ali 45
The Man Who Insulted Abu Hurairah 46
Those Who Attempted to Remove Abu Bakr and 'Umar from Their Graves 46
The Couple Who Fornicated on the Day of 'Arafah 48
The Woman Who Lied on Sa'id ibn Zayd 48
Al-Hajjaj ibn Yusuf's Killing of Sa'id ibn Jubayr 49
Amir 'Abdul Aziz bin Mutaib al-Rashid's Killing of the Poor and Weak 52
Innovators Who Slandered the People of Sunnah 54
Ismaili Shias 55

Punishments Less Than Death 56
The Tyrant Who Intended Evil with the Wife of Ibrahim 56
The Owner of the Two Gardens 59
Owners of the Garden Who Denied the Poor from the Garden 60
The Leper and the Bald Man 62
Those Who Belittled the Sanctity of Mecca and the Ka'bah 66
The Abducted Boy at the Ka'bah 67
The Man and the Antelope 68
The Man Who Lied on His Wife 69
Meccan Boycott of the Hashemites 70
The Man Who Opposed the Command of the Prophet 70
The Man Who Belittled an Authentic Hadith 71
Those Who Insulted the Companions 75
Worldly Punishment for Backbiting 79
The Man Who Harassed the Imam While He Prayed 79
The Couples Who Wife-Swapped 80
The Man Who Harmed 'Uthman's Wife 81
The Youth Who Harmed the Bird 81
Those Who Harmed the Scholars 82
The Punishment of Busr ibn Abi Artat 84
Those Who Said the Qur'an Was Created 84
Punishment Which Occurred After Death 85
Punishments the Prophet Saw During the Night Journey 86
Punishments the Prophet Saw While Dreaming 89
Punishments Upon Individuals 93
The Continuous Punishment of Abu Jahl 101
The Continuous Punishment of 'Ubay ibn Khalaf 102
The Man Who Disrespected His Mother 104
Fire Within Graves 104
The Woman Who Died Disobeying Her Husband 106
The Woman Who Died Persistent Upon Three Sins 107
Fire from the Casket of the Shia 110

The Woman Who Delayed the Prayer and Spied on Her Neighbors...... 112
The Deceased with a Ring of Fire Around His Neck 113
The Man Who Sinned While in Seclusion.. 115
The Man Who Performed Hajj with Pilfered Wealth 115
The Man Who Insulted the Companions 116
'Ubaydullah ibn Ziyad, the Killer of Husayn ibn 'Ali 116
The Deceased with Iron Nails in His Body 117
Deceased Turned Away from the Qibla in Their Graves 117
Those Who Died Upon Other Than the Sunnah 118
Those Who Died Addicted to Smoking 118
Moans from the Grave 120
Punishments Seen in Dreams and Unconsciousness............................ 121
Al-Hajjaj ibn Yusuf's Punishment.. 122
Bishr al-Marisi 123
Ibn Abi Dawud the Mu'tazilite 123
The Man Who Denied the Divine Decree 124
Those Who Believed in the Unity of Existence 124
The Obligation of Believing in the Bliss and Punishment of the Grave .. 125
Stories of the Deceased Who Were Honored After Death.................... 126
The Story of Daniel 126
The Story of 'Abdullah ibn At-Thamir.. 128
'Umar ibn al-Khattab After Death 129
The Bodies of the Martyrs 130
Talha ibn 'Ubaydullah.. 132
Martyrs from the Battle of al-Yamamah 132
Sa'd ibn Mu'adh 134
Abu Muhammad al-Barbahari 134
A Small Graveyard in Riyadh... 135
Sweet-Scented Plants Inside the Grave 136
The Scent of Perfume from a Dream.. 136
Conclusion 137

Biography of Author

Birth and Lineage

He is the noble scholar Shaykh Hamūd ibn 'Abdullāh ibn Hamūd al-Tuwaijri ﷺ. He is from the well-known Arabian tribe of Anezzah. This tribe is from the largest tribes on the Arabian Peninsula. In 1915 (1334 AH) after the migration, he was born in Sudayr, a historical region in Najd, in central Saudi Arabia.

His Studies

He began seeking knowledge as a youth. His father died when he was eight years old, and he memorized the Noble Qur'ān at the age of ten. During this time, he also studied books of *tawhīd*, hadīth, Islāmic jurisprudence, and grammar. When he became a young man, the shaykh constantly sat in the lessons of the noble scholar and judge of Sudayr, Shaykh 'Abdullāh ibn 'Abdul 'Azīz al-Angarie. He remained with him for 25 years, and would read to him the books of *tawhīd*, *tafsīr*, hadīth, Islāmic jurisprudence, Arabic grammar, and history. The books he studied with his shaykh include *Commentary on Sahīh al-Bukhārī* by Ibn Hajar, *Al-Mughni* by Ibn Qudamah, *Methodology of the Prophetic Sunnah* by Ibn Taymiyyah, *The Rejection of the Conflict Between Reason and Reve-*

lation by Ibn Taymiyyah, *Major Egyptian Fatwas* by Ibn Taymiyyah, and *Provisions for the Hereafter* by Ibn al-Qayyim.

During this study, he memorized a great number of texts; thus, he completely understood all that he read. His shaykh gave him *ijazah*, authorization to transmit and teach numerous books, such as *Sahīh al-Bukhārī* and *Sahīh Muslim*, the collections of Tirmidhī and Abū Dāwūd, and the musnad of Imām Ahmad, along with the books of Ibn Taymiyyah and Ibn al-Qayyim.

Shaykh Hamūd also studied under the noble scholar Shaykh Muhammad ibn 'Abdul Muhsin al-Khayāl, the former judge of Madinah, where he studied grammar and Islāmic inheritance jurisprudence. He studied under Shaykh Sulayman ibn Hamdan, a former judge in Mecca, learning Hanbali jurisprudence. Both scholars, likewise, gave Shaykh Hamūd *ijazah* in all the well-known books of hadīth.

Shaykh Hamūd was appointed judge of the Eastern Province in 1368 AH, after the migration and coinciding with the year 1949. He remained in this position until 1372 AH, when he was granted release from his position, upon request.

During the end of his life, Shaykh Hamūd would spend his days studying and researching until 'Ishā prayer. He would spend his nights performing the night prayer, whether traveling or at home.

His Works

Shaykh Hamūd authored over 50 books. He would read his books of refutations to the noble scholar, and former grand mufti of Saudi Arabia, Shaykh Muhammad Ibrāhīm 'Ālī Shaykh. Shaykh Muhammad would say about Shaykh Hamūd, "Shaykh Hamūd is a mujāhid, may Allāh reward him with good!"

His Students

Shaykh Hamūd granted *ijazah* to a number of scholars, including Shaykh Rabīʿ al-Madhkalī, Shaykh Sālih ibn Humayd, Shaykh Sālih bin ʿAbdul ʿAzīz ʿĀlī Shaykh, and others.

Shaykh Rabīʿ said about him, "It is incumbent upon the youth of this land to benefit from the books of this noble and truthful Salafī Shaykh. He spent his life in calling to the truth and defending the Sunnah of the Messenger ﷺ against innovation and misguidance. He has a lofty status in this land. By Allāh, we have not given him his just due, nor benefited from the books on this man."[1]

His Character

Shaykh Hamūd did not like to rely upon anyone, even his relatives. His sons said that he would not ask anyone for anything at all, even after his health declined. He would make his own tea and coffee, although his children would insist that he rest his body and allow them to prepare it for him. While traveling, Shaykh Hamūd would serve and tend to his travel companions, even when he became elderly. The Shaykh would also prepare meals. Despite this, it was his normal habit to spend his nights in prayer. He would lie on his side shortly before Fajr prayer; then, heat his water for *wudhū*.

---

[1] Translator's note: Taken from a lecture entitled "Pearls of Salafiyyah" by Shaykh Rabīʿ.

His Death

Prior to his death, Shaykh Hamūd gave his eldest son everything he owned to give away in charity. Because he abstained from the worldly life, he did not possess much. Shaykh Hamūd died in the month of Jumādā al-Awwal during the year 1413 AH, after the migration, and coinciding with the year 1992.

بِسْمِ اللَّـهِ الرَّحْمَـٰنِ الرَّحِيمِ

Destruction of Previous Nations

Indeed, all the praises belong to Allāh. We praise Him, we seek His aid, we seek His forgiveness, and we repent to Him. We seek refuge with Allāh from the evil of our souls and from our evil actions. Whosoever Allāh guides, none can misguide. And whoever He misguides, there is no guide for them. I testify that nothing has the right to be worshipped except Allāh, alone, without partners, and I testify that Muhammad is His slave and messenger, sent as a mercy to the creation. May the salutations of Allāh and peace be upon him, his family, his companions, and those who follow them in goodness until the Day of Judgment.

As to what follows, indeed, Allāh ﷻ has narrated information to us in His Book concerning those who belied the messengers. He ﷻ informed us that He destroyed them due to their sins and disobeying the messengers. In these stories, Allāh ﷻ gives lessons to those who possess intellect and admonitions for those who possess piety.

The punishments sent down upon them varied according to the crimes. Allāh ﷻ informed us of this in His statement:

﴿ فَكُلًّا أَخَذْنَا بِذَنبِهِۦ فَمِنْهُم مَّنْ أَرْسَلْنَا عَلَيْهِ حَاصِبًا وَمِنْهُم مَّنْ أَخَذَتْهُ الصَّيْحَةُ وَمِنْهُم مَّنْ خَسَفْنَا بِهِ الْأَرْضَ وَمِنْهُم مَّنْ أَغْرَقْنَا ۚ وَمَا كَانَ اللَّهُ لِيَظْلِمَهُمْ وَلَٰكِن كَانُوا أَنفُسَهُمْ يَظْلِمُونَ ﴿٤٠﴾ ﴾

So, each We seized for his sin; and among them were those upon whom We sent a storm of stones, and among them were those who were seized by a loud scream [from the sky], and among them were those whom We caused the earth to swallow, and among them were those whom We drowned. And Allāh would not have wronged them, but it was they who were wronging themselves.[2]

As for the people of Nūh, then Allāh ﷻ drowned them with the flood that afflicted the earth. No one was spared except Nūh ﵇ and those with him aboard the ark. As for the people of 'Ād, they were destroyed by a furious, violent wind. The people of Thamūd were destroyed by a loud scream. This was a tremendous shout which annihilated them such that they laid dead, prostrate in their homes. As for the people of Lūt, Allāh ﷻ turned their cities upside down such that the top became the bottom, and He ﷻ rained on them stones of baked clay, piled up. As for the people of Shu'aīb, the torment of the day of shadow seized them. They were destroyed by the great scream, and laid dead, prostrate in their homes. As for Pharaoh and his followers, indeed, Allāh ﷻ drowned them in the river and none of them survived. As it relates to Qārūn, Allāh ﷻ caused the earth to swallow him and his home. Those who transgressed in the matter of the Sabbath, indeed, Allāh ﷻ transformed them into monkeys, while He transformed others from the Children of

[2] Sūrah al-'Ankabūt, 29:40.

Israel into swine. As for the people of Sab'ā, Allāh ﷻ released upon them the flood of the dam, and it shredded everything into pieces. Those from the Children of Israel who caused corruption in the land and behaved with arrogance, Allāh ﷻ sent against them Sennacherib, and then Nebuchadnezzar.[3] They entered the very innermost parts of their homes and destroyed, with total destruction, what they took.[4]

As for the army of the elephants, Allāh ﷻ said about them:

﴿ وَأَرْسَلَ عَلَيْهِمْ طَيْرًا أَبَابِيلَ ۝٣ تَرْمِيهِم بِحِجَارَةٍ مِّن سِجِّيلٍ ۝٤ فَجَعَلَهُمْ كَعَصْفٍ مَّأْكُولٍ ۝٥ ﴾

> **And sent against them birds in flocks, striking them with stones of hard clay, and He made them like eaten straw.**[5]

---

[3] Translator's note: Allāh ﷻ said, "So, when the promise came for the first of the two, We sent against you slaves of Ours, given to terrible warfare. They entered the very innermost parts of your homes. And it was a promise (completely) fulfilled." Sūrah al-Isrā, 17:5.

[4] Translator's note: Allāh ﷻ said, "Then, when the second promise came to pass, (We permitted your enemies) to make your faces sorrowful and to enter the mosque (of Jerusalem) as they had entered it before, and to destroy with utter destruction all that fell in their hands." Sūrah al-Isrā, 17:7.

[5] Sūrah al-Fīl, 105:3-5.

The Muslim Nation's Protection from Complete Eradication

If you understand this, then also understand that Allāh ﷻ exempted the ummah of Muhammad ﷺ from the punishment of eradication. This was done as an honor to His Prophet ﷺ and as a response to his supplication. Thauban ؓ narrated the Messenger of Allāh ﷺ said:

وَإِنِّي سَأَلْتُ رَبِّي لأُمَّتِي أَنْ لاَ يُهْلِكَهَا بِسَنَةٍ بِعَامَّةٍ وَأَنْ لاَ يُسَلِّطَ عَلَيْهِمْ عَدُوًّا مِنْ سِوَى أَنْفُسِهِمْ فَيَسْتَبِيحَ بَيْضَتَهُمْ وَإِنَّ رَبِّي قَالَ يَا مُحَمَّدُ إِنِّي إِذَا قَضَيْتُ قَضَاءً فَإِنَّهُ لاَ يُرَدُّ وَإِنِّي أَعْطَيْتُكَ لأُمَّتِكَ أَنْ لاَ أُهْلِكَهُمْ بِسَنَةٍ بِعَامَّةٍ وَأَنْ لاَ أُسَلِّطَ عَلَيْهِمْ عَدُوًّا مِنْ سِوَى أَنْفُسِهِمْ يَسْتَبِيحُ بَيْضَتَهُمْ وَلَوِ اجْتَمَعَ عَلَيْهِمْ مَنْ بِأَقْطَارِهَا حَتَّى يَكُونَ بَعْضُهُمْ يُهْلِكُ بَعْضًا وَيَسْبِي بَعْضُهُمْ بَعْضًا

I begged my Lord that my ummah should not be destroyed because of famine, nor be dominated by an enemy who is not amongst them that will take over their society and positions of authority. And my Lord said, "Muhammad, whenever I make a decision, there is none to change it. I grant you for your ummah that it would not be destroyed by famine, and it would not be dominated by an enemy who would not be amongst it and would take over their society and positions of authority, even if all the people from the different parts of the world join hands together (for this purpose). Rather, the enemy would come from amongst themselves, such that some people would kill some and imprison others.[6]

[6] Sahīh Muslim, 2889.

The Messenger of Allāh ﷺ said:

سألت ربي عزّ وجلّ أربعاً فأعطاني ثلاثاً ومنعني واحدة. سألت الله أن لا يجمع أمتي على ضلالة فأعطانيها, وسألت الله أن لا يظهر عليهم عدواً من غيرهم فأعطانيها, وسألت الله أن لا يهلكهم بالسنين كما أهلك الأمم قبلهم فأعطانيها, وسألت الله عزّ وجلّ أن لا يلبسهم شيعاً وأن لا يذيق بعضهم بأس بعض فمنعنيها

I asked my Lord ﷻ for four things. He granted me three and denied me one. I asked Allāh that my nation not unite upon misguidance and He granted me this. And I asked Allāh that He not grant an enemy from outside our ranks victory over us, so He granted me this. I asked Allāh that He not destroy us with famine like He destroyed the previous nations, and He granted me this. And I asked Allāh ﷻ not to allow my nation to break into factions, causing them to taste the harm of each other, but He denied me this.[7]

In a narration from Abū Hurairah ؓ, the Prophet ﷺ said:

وسألته أن لا يعذبهم بما عذب به الأمم قبلهم فأعطانيها

And I asked Him not to punish them with the punishment given to the previous nations, and He granted me this.[8]

Khabbab ibn al-Aratt ؓ narrated the Prophet ﷺ said:

سألت ربي عزّ وجلّ أن لا يهلكنا بما أهلك به الأمم قبلنا فأعطانيه

I asked my Lord ﷻ not to destroy us in the way He destroyed the nations prior to us, and He granted me this.[9]

---

[7] Collected by Ahmad.

[8] Collected by At-Tabarāni.

The Messenger of Allāh ﷺ said:

سألت ربي أن لا يهلك أمتي بالسنة فأعطانيها

I asked my Lord not to destroy my ummah with famine, and He granted that to me.[10]

PUNISHMENTS UPON INDIVIDUALS FROM PREVIOUS NATIONS AND THIS NATION

If you understand that Allāh ﷻ has removed the punishment of eradication from the ummah of Muhammad ﷺ, then also understand that the punishments sent upon individuals from previous nations are numerous and of various types.

These punishments are of two categories. One: the punishment in this worldly life; and two: the punishment after death.

The punishment in this worldly life is of two categories. One: the punishment that leads to death; and two: the punishment that contains harm which is less than death. There are many stories from both categories.

---

[9] Collected by Ahmad and Tirmidhī.
[10] Collected by Muslim and Ahmad.

THE MAN WHO DRAGGED HIS GARMENT OUT OF PRIDE AND ARROGANCE

From the stories included in the first category—worldly punishments in this world that lead to death, from the previous nations—is the story of the man who arrogantly dragged his garment. He was amazed with himself, so Allāh ﷻ caused the earth to swallow him. This story is mentioned in several hadīth.

Ibn 'Umar ﷺ said the Messenger of Allāh ﷺ said:

بَيْنَمَا رَجُلٌ يَجُرُّ إِزَارَهُ مِنَ الْخُيَلاَءِ خُسِفَ بِهِ، فَهُوَ يَتَجَلْجَلُ فِي الأَرْضِ إِلَى يَوْمِ الْقِيَامَةِ

While a man was dragging his lower garment out of pride, the earth swallowed him up and he will continue sinking into the earth until the Day of Resurrection.[11]

Abū Hurairah ﷺ narrated the Messenger of Allāh ﷺ said:

بَيْنَا رَجُلٌ يَتَبَخْتَرُ فِي حُلَّةٍ ، مُعْجَبٌ بِجُمَّتِهِ ، قَدْ أَسْبَلَ إِزَارَهُ ، إِذْ خَسَفَ اللَّهُ بِهِ ، فَهُوَ يَتَجَلْجَلُ – أَوْ قَالَ : يَهْوِي – فِيهَا إِلَى يَوْمِ الْقِيَامَةِ

While a man was strutting in his two-piece garment, impressed with his shoulder-length hair as he dragged his garment, Allāh caused the earth to swallow him. He will continue to sink until the Day of Judgment.[12]

---

[11] Bukhārī, 5345 and Muslim, 3894.
[12] Collected in Ahmad and Ibn Habban.

The Messenger of Allāh ﷺ said:

إن رجلاً ممن كان قبلكم كان يتبختر في حلة له قد أعجبته جمته وبرداه إذ خسف به الأرض فهو يتجلجل فيها حتى تقوم الساعة

A man from those who lived prior to you was strutting in his two-piece garment, impressed by his shoulder-length hair and cloak, when suddenly, the earth swallowed him. He will continue to sink in it until the Hour is established.[13]

The Prophet ﷺ said:

بينا رجل فيمن كان قبلكم خرج في بردين أخضرين يختال فيهما أمر الله الأرض فأخذته وإنه ليتجلجل فيها إلى يوم القيامة

A man from those who lived prior to you went out arrogantly wearing two green cloaks. Allāh commanded the earth to seize him. And he will continue to sink until the Day of Judgment.[14]

The Man and Woman Who Violated the Sanctity of the Sacred Ka'bah

From the stories included in the first category—worldly punishments in this world that lead to death, from the previous nations—are the many stories of those who belittled the sanctity of the sacred Ka'bah. Included in this is the story of Isāf and Nā'ila. Ibn Ishāq said, "It was narrated by

[13] Collected in Sahīh Muslim.
[14] Collected in Ahmad.

'Ā'ishah ﷺ that she said, 'We continued to hear about Isāf and Nā'ila, a man and woman from the tribe of Jurhum. He was Isāf ibn Bagha and she was Nā'ila bint Dhib. Isāf committed adultery with Nā'ila inside the Ka'bah; thus, Allāh transformed them into two stones.'" The chain of narration is authentic.

Muhammad ibn Ishāq said, "The tribe of Jurhum violated the sanctity of the sacred city of Mecca. A man and woman entered the Ka'bah and committed adultery inside. Others say he only kissed her inside the Ka'bah. They were both transformed into stones. The man's name was Isāf ibn Bagha and the woman's name was Nā'ila bint Dhib. They were both removed from the Ka'bah. One of them was propped up at Safā and the other was propped up at Marwa. They were only placed there to serve as a reminder and warning for the people against violating the Ka'bah, as it would be a deterrent when the people saw them. The pilgrims would wipe these two stones while standing at Safā and Marwa until they became effaced. Then, these two stones became idols that were worshipped. When Qusaī ibn Kilab became king of Mecca, he moved the stones from Safā and Marwa. He attached one to the Ka'bah and the other he placed at the Zamzam well. The pilgrims would sacrifice at these two stones. The people during the pre-Islāmic times would pass by Isāf and Nā'ila and wipe them. They remained until the conquest of Mecca, when the Messenger of Allāh ﷺ shattered them, along with the rest of the idols."

Al-Azraqī[15] narrated that 'Amra[16] said, "Isāf and Nā'ila were a man and a woman who were transformed into stone. They were removed from the

---

[15] Translator's note: Muhammad ibn 'Abd Allāh al-Azraqī was an Islamic historian from the 9th century.

[16] Translator's note: She is 'Amra bint 'Abdur Rahmān ibn Sa'd.

inside of the Ka'bah and their clothes were still on them after their transformation. One of them was placed beside the Ka'bah, while the other was placed at the well of Zamzam. The pagans would bring gifts to them like they brought gifts to the Ka'bah. The place of the stone was at the low wall beside the Ka'bah, called Hatīm. The stones were originally placed to serve as a warning to the people, but as time went on the people began to worship them. When the clothes of the idols wore out, the pagans would replace their clothes. The idols beside the Ka'bah were placed alongside the idol at the well of Zamzam. The pagans would sacrifice at these two idols."

THE MAN WHO STOLE FROM THE KA'BAH

From the stories of those who belittled the sanctity of the Ka'bah is what has been narrated by Ibn Abī Shaība from 'Abdur Rahmān ibn Sābit, that he said, "During the pre-Islāmic days of ignorance, the people would all leave during the religious season, and no one would remain behind in Mecca. Once, a man, who was a thief, stayed behind. He intended to steal some gold from inside the Ka'bah. When he entered his head inside the Ka'bah, it squeezed him. When the people returned, they found his head inside the sacred house while his torso was outside. They threw his body to the dogs and cleaned the Ka'bah."[17]

[17] The Musannaf of Ibn Abī Shaybah, 14095.

The Gang of Men Who Attempted to Rob the Ka'bah

Al-Azraqī mentioned in *The News of Mecca*, narrated from Ibn Ishāq, that he said, "The house (Ka'bah) used to contain treasures inside its cavity. The people would toss their jewelry and wealth inside, and during this time the treasures belonged to a bishop. Five men from the tribe of Jurhum made a pact to steal the treasures. Four of the men climbed on a corner of the Ka'bah (to act as lookouts), while the fifth man broke inside. Allāh ﷻ inverted it and the man inside fell upside down and died. The other four fled."[18]

Men Who Pledged a False Oath at the Ka'bah

Translator's note: Al-Qasāmah is a practice from the pre-Islāmic days of ignorance. When a person was murdered and there were no witnesses, but there was evidence pointing to a particular person as the perpetrator, the family of the slain would give the oath of al-Qasāmah. This was the oath taken by 50 men from the relatives of the slain person by saying, individually, "I swear by Allāh that so-and-so murdered so-and-so." Likewise, 50 men from the relatives of the accused could take an oath declaring his innocence. End of translator's note.

It was narrated by Al-Azraqī, from 'Abdullāh ibn Abī Najīh, from his father, that he said, "During the pre-Islāmic days of ignorance, 50 men

[18] Al-Azraqī, *The News of Mecca*, 1/88.

gathered at the Ka'bah and made an oath of Al-Qasāmah, but their oath was false and a lie. As they traveled back home, they took the midday nap beneath a boulder. While they slept, the boulder turned over on top of them. As they crawled from underneath the boulder, it broke into 50 pieces. Each of the 50 men was hit with a piece of the boulder, killing them all. The men were from the tribe of Lu'ayy ibn Ghālib."[19]

The Man Who Belittled the Du'a at the Ka'bah

Qusaī ibn Kilab, the 5th generation grandfather of the Prophet ﷺ, held the Ka'bah in high regard. The tribe of Quraysh, who came after him, also venerated the Ka'bah. For this reason, the people hated to make an oath at the sacred house, fearing they would be punished with regard to their lives and wealth. Rabī'ah ibn al-Hārith ﷺ said, "During the pre-Islāmic days of ignorance, a man from the Tribe of Kinānah attacked and assaulted his cousin, oppressing him. The oppressed cousin implored him by Allāh and their bond of kinship to stop oppressing him, but the man refused and continued to oppress him. The oppressed cousin said, 'I swear by Allāh, I will travel to the Ka'bah during the sacred month and supplicate to Allāh against you.' The oppressive cousin mockingly replied, 'This is my she-camel. I will sit you on her back myself. So go and supplicate as much as you can!' Thus, he gave him his camel and the man left, heading to Mecca during the sacred month. Upon reaching the Ka'bah, the oppressed cousin said, 'O Allāh, I call upon You with the supplication of one who is in need. Send to my

[19] Collected by As-Suyūtī in *Ad Dar*, 2/556.

cousin a disease that has no cure.' Then he left and returned to his cousin and found that his stomach had expanded like a leather bowl. It continued to expand until it burst." Rabī'ah ibn al-Hārith ﷺ continued, "I narrated this hadīth to Ibn 'Abbās ﷺ and he said, 'I saw an oppressed man who supplicated against his cousin that he would lose his eyesight, and I saw the oppressive cousin being lead around in a group of the blind.'"[20]

THE THIEF WHO GAVE FALSE OATH AT THE STATION OF IBRAHIM

It has been narrated with a chain attributed to Ibn 'Abbās ﷺ that he said, "A man went out in search of his young camel in the sacred area of Masjid Haram. He began calling out for his camel. The thief said, 'You are a liar. You don't have a camel here.' The owner of the camel said, 'Swear by Allāh to what you are saying.' The thief said, 'I will swear by Allāh!' So, the thief stood at the station of Ibrāhīm and said, 'I swear by Allāh, the Creator of this house, that you don't have a camel here.' It was said to the owner of the camel, 'There is nothing more you can do.' The owner of the camel stood between the Yemeni corner and the station of Ibrāhīm and raised his hands in supplication against the thief and then he left. The thief lost his intellect and became insane. The thief walked through Mecca screaming, 'My wealth and the camels belong to the owner of the camels!' This news reached 'Abdul Muttalib, so he gathered up his young camels and gave them to the camel owner.

[20] Al-Azraqī, *The News of Mecca*, 2/25.

The thief continued to wander about until he fell from a mountain and the beasts of prey ate him."[21]

ABRAHA, THE AKSUMITE ARMY GENERAL WHO INTENDED TO DESTROY THE KA'BAH

Abraha was a general in modern day Ethiopia and Eritrea, who took a flock of elephants to Mecca to destroy the Ka'bah. Allāh ﷻ sent a flock of birds against the army. The birds struck the army with stones of hard clay, killing them. Abraha fled and was not hit with stones, but he was afflicted with something within his body more damaging than the stones that struck his army. Ibn Ishāq said, "Abraha's body was injured, so they carried him away. His fingertips began to fall off one by one, followed by blood and pus flowing from his body. By the time he reached the city of San'ā, he resembled a baby chickling. He did not die until his heart and chest split open."

THE WRETCHED MAN WHO STOLE THE BLACK STONE

From the stories of those who violated the sanctity of the Ka'bah is the story of the filthy, despicable person named Abū Tāhir al-Qarmatī,[22] may Allāh ﷻ curse him. He entered Mecca during the days of Hajj, in

---

[21] Al-Azraqī, *The News of Mecca*, 2/26.

[22] Translator's note: The Qarmatians were a syncretic branch of Sevener Ismaili Shia.

the year 317, after the migration, and killed numerous pilgrims performing Hajj at Masjid al-Haram. He stole the people's wealth. He stole the black stone and the door of the Ka'bah and returned it to his homeland. Abū al-Fidā said, "When Abū Tāhir al-Qarmatī returned home, Allāh ﷻ afflicted him with gangrenous sores on his body. He suffered for a long time and his limbs were severed. He watched as worms ate away at his flesh."[23]

It is mentioned in both *The Complete History* by Ibn al-Athīr[24] and *The Beginning and the End* by Ibn Kathīr that Abū Tāhir al-Qarmatī, may Allāh ﷻ curse him, ordered a man to climb up to the gutter of the Ka'bah and remove it. When the man climbed up, he fell on his head and died. When this happened, the filthy Abū Tāhir left the gutter alone.

There are numerous stories about those punished for disrespecting the sanctity of the Ka'bah, more than what we have mentioned. However, in those stories the punishment did not result in death. Therefore, we did not mention them here. These stories will be mentioned in the second category, in shaa Allāh.

---

[23] *Al-Bidayah wa Nihayah.*

[24] Translator's note: Ibn al-Athīr was a famous Muslim historian. He died in the year 73 AH.

THOSE WHO MOCKED THE MESSENGER OF ALLAH

Also, from the stories of those in the first category are those who mocked the Messenger of Allāh ﷺ. They were afflicted with various punishments.

THE FIVE CHIEFTAINS WHO MOCKED THE MESSENGER OF ALLAH

It has been narrated by Al-Bayhaqī in his book *Evidence of Prophecy*, from Sa'īd ibn Jubayr, from Ibn 'Abbās ﷺ, concerning the Qur'ānic verse:

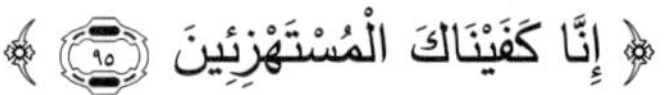

Truly! We will suffice you against the scoffers.[25]

"The scoffers mentioned in this verse are Al-Walīd ibn al-Mughīrah, Al-Aswad ibn 'Abdu Yaghūth, Al-Aswad ibn al-Muttalib, Al-Hārith ibn Qays, and Al-'Ās ibn Wā'il. Jibrīl came to the Messenger of Allāh ﷺ when he was performing tawāf around the House (Ka'bah). He stood and the Messenger of Allāh stood next to him. Al-Aswad ibn 'Abdu Yaghūth passed by and Jibrīl pointed to his stomach, which swelled up, and he died of dropsy. Al-Walīd ibn al-Mughīrah passed by, and Jibrīl pointed at a wound on the lower part of his ankle, which he had gotten

[25] Sūrah al-Hijr, 15:95.

two years earlier when he was trailing his garment and passed by a man who was feathering his arrows. One of the arrows got caught in his garment and scratched his foot. It was an insignificant wound, but now it opened again, and he died of it. Al-'Ās ibn Wā'il passed by, and Jibrīl pointed to the instep of his foot. Al-'Ās set off on his donkey, heading for At-Tā'if. He rested by a thorny tree, a thorn pierced his foot, and he died from it. Al-Hārith ibn Qays passed by, and Jibrīl pointed at his head. It filled with pus and killed him."[26]

"As for Al-Aswad ibn al-Muttalib, he sat down for an evening chat and then began to shout, 'O my tribe, will you not protect me? He is trying to kill me!' They responded, 'We do not see anything.' He said, 'O my tribe, will you not keep him away from me? This is him, right here, he is poking my eye out with a thorn!' They responded, 'We do not see anything.' He continued to scream for help until he went blind. He then began banging his head against the wall until he died."

It was mentioned in both *Genealogies of the Nobles* by Al-Balādhurī[27] and *The Complete History* by Ibn al-Athīr that when Al-Aswad ibn 'Abdu Yaghūth would see the poor Muslims, he would mockingly say to his companions, "These are the kings of the earth that will inherit the kingdoms of Khosrow and Caesar!" And he used to say to the Prophet ﷺ, "Did you not speak to someone from the heavens today, O Muhammad?"

Al-Balādhurī and Ibn al-Athīr mentioned that Al-Aswad ibn al-Muttalib and his companions used to wink, clap, and whistle at the Prophet ﷺ and his companions while saying, "The king of the earth has

---

[26] *Tafsīr ibn Kathīr* and Sūrah al-Hijr, 15:95.

[27] Translator's note: Ahmad ibn Yahyā ibn Jābir al-Balādhurī was a Muslim historian. He died in the year 279 AH.

come to you, and those who will conquer the treasures of Khosrow and Caesar."

WARNING TO THOSE WHO MOCK HADITH

If you understand the punishments that befell those who mocked the Messenger of Allāh ﷺ, then also understand that it is feared that those who mock the authentic hadīth narrated from the Prophet ﷺ, they will be afflicted with the same punishments that befell those before them.

And know, mocking the Prophet ﷺ includes mocking anything from his manners, statements, or actions. This applies to those who mock the authentic hadīth, such as those arrogant, foolish people who think too highly of themselves and their mistake-filled writings. These individuals make their flawed intellects and evil opinions as a scale to judge the hadīth. Thus, whatever agrees with their intellects, they accept and promote it, even if the narration is fabricated or weak. And whatever contradicts their intellects or opinions, they throw it against the wall and reject it, even if it is collected in *Sahīh Bukhārī* and *Sahīh Muslim*. This methodology is similar to what was mentioned by Al-Balādhurī and Ibn al-Athīr concerning the disbelievers from the Quraysh who belied and mocked what their intellects could not comprehend from the revelation. Therefore, when the Prophet ﷺ informed them that the Muslims would conquer Khosrow and Caesar, and take their treasures, they rejected it because they could not conceive it.

The Prophet ﷺ said:

مَنْ تَشَبَّهَ بِقَوْمٍ فَهُوَ مِنْهُمْ

Whoever resembles a people is from them.[28]

Therefore, those who belittle the authentic hadīth of the Prophet ﷺ and reject them with their intellects and opinions are not safe from being afflicted with a punishment to serve as a lesson for others. And you know rejecting authentic hadīth from the Prophet ﷺ, and opposing them with opinions and intellect, is not a light matter. So how about those who belittle the hadīth and clearly proclaim their opposition to them! This affair is extremely dangerous. It is feared that those who do this are apostates from Islām.

What is worse than that is how some of the wretched people of our era reject the narrations. A student of knowledge had a discussion with one of these worthless individuals concerning an authentic hadīth collected in *Sahīh Muslim* that opposed the opinion of this individual. He said to the student of knowledge, "Put this hadīth beneath your foot!" This is clear apostasy. If there were any Islām within this wretched person, then his Islām would have prevented him using this terrible statement to reject a hadīth authentically narrated from the Prophet ﷺ. We complain to Allāh ﷻ about the evil of this wretched person and those similar to him from the heretics, those who have misled numerous people from the straight path.

﴿وَإِذَا قِيلَ لَهُمْ لَا تُفْسِدُوا فِي الْأَرْضِ قَالُوا إِنَّمَا نَحْنُ مُصْلِحُونَ ﴿١١﴾ أَلَا
إِنَّهُمْ هُمُ الْمُفْسِدُونَ وَلَٰكِن لَّا يَشْعُرُونَ ﴿١٢﴾﴾

And when it is said to them, "Make not mischief on the earth," they say, 'We are only peacemakers.' Verily!

[28] Sunan Abi Dāwūd, 4031.

They are the ones who make mischief, but they perceive not.'"[29]

Imām Ahmad ﷺ said, "Whoever rejects a hadīth from the Messenger of Allāh ﷺ, then he is on the verge of destruction."[30]

Al-Hasan ibn 'Ālī al-Barbahārī[31] said in *Explanation of the Sunnah*, "If you see a man criticizing the narrations and not accepting them, or rejecting anything from the information of the Messenger of Allāh ﷺ, then doubt his Islām. For indeed, he is a man with an evil methodology and speech. And, in reality, he is insulting the Messenger of Allāh ﷺ and his companions."

Al-Barbahārī said, "No one who prays towards the Qibla of Islām exits from Islām until he rejects a verse from the Book of Allāh ﷻ, or he rejects anything from the narrations of the Messenger of Allāh ﷺ, or he prays to other than Allāh ﷻ, or sacrifices to other than Allāh. If any of this occurs, then it is obligatory for you to believe that this person has exited Islām."

Al-Barbahārī said, "Whoever rejects a verse from the Book of Allāh, then he has indeed rejected the Book, all of it. And whoever rejects a hadīth from the Messenger of Allāh ﷺ, then he has indeed rejected all the narrations, and he is a disbeliever in Allāh ﷻ."

Also, Al-Barbahārī said, "There is nothing between the individual and him becoming a disbeliever except that he rejects anything which Allāh ﷻ sent down, or he adds to the speech of Allāh or subtracts from

---

[29] Sūrah al-Baqarah, 2:11-12.

[30] *History of the Hanbalites.*

[31] Translator's note: He is the scholar Al-Hasan ibn 'Ālī al-Barbahārī. He died 329 years after migration.

it, or that he denies something Allāh ﷻ said, or anything from the speech of the Messenger of Allāh ﷺ."

Al-Barbahārī also said, "If you hear a man criticizing the narrations, or rejecting the narrations, or preferring something over the narrations, then doubt his Islām; but do not doubt that he is a person of desires and an innovator."

Al-Barbahārī said, "If you hear of a man who does not want the hadīth when it is given to him, but he wants the Qur'ān, then do not doubt that he is a man upon heresy.

Also, Al-Barbahārī said, "Whoever rejects or doubts a letter from the Qur'ān, or anything brought by the Messenger of Allāh ﷺ, he will meet Allāh ﷻ as a denier."

The statement that the person who rejects any hadīth from the Messenger of Allāh ﷺ is a disbeliever is proven by the statement of Allāh ﷻ:

﴿ فَلَا وَرَبِّكَ لَا يُؤْمِنُونَ حَتَّىٰ يُحَكِّمُوكَ فِيمَا شَجَرَ بَيْنَهُمْ ثُمَّ لَا يَجِدُوا فِي أَنفُسِهِمْ حَرَجًا مِّمَّا قَضَيْتَ وَيُسَلِّمُوا تَسْلِيمًا ﴿٦٥﴾ ﴾

But no, by your Lord, they can have no faith until they make you (O Muhammad) judge in all disputes between them, and find in themselves no resistance against your decisions, and accept (them) with full submission.[32]

[32] Sūrah an-Nisā', 4:65.

Allāh ﷻ swore to His Holiness that there is no faith for the person who does not make the Messenger ﷺ the judge in his affairs, and is pleased with the judgment, and submits to it completely. Allāh ﷻ said:

﴿ وَمَن يُشَاقِقِ الرَّسُولَ مِن بَعْدِ مَا تَبَيَّنَ لَهُ الْهُدَىٰ وَيَتَّبِعْ غَيْرَ سَبِيلِ
الْمُؤْمِنِينَ نُوَلِّهِ مَا تَوَلَّىٰ وَنُصْلِهِ جَهَنَّمَ ۖ وَسَاءَتْ مَصِيرًا ﴿١١٥﴾ ﴾

And whoever contradicts and opposes the Messenger after the right path has been shown clearly to him, and follows other than the believers' way, We shall keep him in the path he has chosen and burn him in Hell—what an evil destination.[33]

Allāh ﷻ said:

﴿ فَلْيَحْذَرِ الَّذِينَ يُخَالِفُونَ عَنْ أَمْرِهِ أَن تُصِيبَهُمْ فِتْنَةٌ أَوْ يُصِيبَهُمْ
عَذَابٌ أَلِيمٌ ﴿٦٣﴾ ﴾

And let those who oppose the Messenger's commandment beware, lest some trial befall them, or a painful torment be inflicted on them.[34]

Imām Ahmad said about this verse, "Do you know what the trial is? The trial is polytheism. Perhaps if he rejects the statement of the Prophet ﷺ some deviance will fall in his heart, and he will be destroyed."

The verses that command obeying the Messenger ﷺ and those that forbid opposing him are numerous. The Prophet ﷺ said:

---

[33] Sūrah an-Nisā', 4:115.
[34] Sūrah an-Nūr, 24:63.

أُمرتُ أن أقاتل الناس حتى يشهدوا أن لا إله إلا الله ويؤمنوا بي وبما جئت به فإذا فعلوا ذلك عصموا مني دماءهم وأموالهم إلا بحقها وحسابهم على الله

I have been commanded to fight the people until they bear witness that there is nothing worthy of worship except Allāh, and they believe in me and what I came with. If they do that, then their blood and wealth are protected from me except in cases dictated by Islāmic law, and their reckoning will be with Allāh.[35]

This is proof for those who declare that those who reject any authentic hadīth from the Prophet ﷺ are disbelievers. This is because the person has left off a condition that makes his blood and wealth sacred. This condition is believing in that which the Messenger ﷺ came with.

Likewise, in order for a person's Islām to be valid, he must testify that Muhammad ﷺ is the Messenger of Allāh. This includes believing in the authentic hadīth from the Prophet ﷺ and completely accepting them. And being far away from rejecting anything from the hadīth with the intellect or opinions.

MEN WHO THREW THE CAMEL AFTERBIRTH ON THE PROPHET WHILE HE WAS PRAYING

Let us return to the stories of those who harmed and belittled the Messenger of Allāh ﷺ and the punishments that befell them in this world, along with what is promised to them from the grievous punishment in

[35] Collected by Muslim from the hadīth of Abū Hurairah.

the Hereafter. From these stories is the story of those who threw camel afterbirth on the back of the Messenger of Allāh ﷺ while he was prostrating. 'Abdullāh ibn Mas'ūd ﷺ said:

بَيْنَمَا رَسُولُ اللَّهِ صلى الله عليه وسلم يُصَلِّي عِنْدَ الْبَيْتِ وَأَبُو جَهْلٍ وَأَصْحَابٌ لَهُ جُلُوسٌ وَقَدْ نُحِرَتْ جَزُورٌ بِالأَمْسِ فَقَالَ أَبُو جَهْلٍ أَيُّكُمْ يَقُومُ إِلَى سَلاَ جَزُورِ بَنِي فُلاَنٍ فَيَأْخُذُهُ فَيَضَعُهُ فِي كَتِفَىْ مُحَمَّدٍ إِذَا سَجَدَ

"While the Messenger of Allāh ﷺ was praying at the Ka'bah, Abū Jahl was sitting nearby with his companions, and a she-camel had been slaughtered the previous day. Abū Jahl said, 'Who will rise to fetch the afterbirth of the she-camel of so-and-so, and place it between the shoulders of Muhammad when he goes down in prostration?'

فَانْبَعَثَ أَشْقَى الْقَوْمِ فَأَخَذَهُ فَلَمَّا سَجَدَ النَّبِيُّ صلى الله عليه وسلم وَضَعَهُ بَيْنَ كَتِفَيْهِ قَالَ فَاسْتَضْحَكُوا وَجَعَلَ بَعْضُهُمْ يَمِيلُ عَلَى بَعْضٍ وَأَنَا قَائِمٌ أَنْظُرُ . لَوْ كَانَتْ لِي مَنَعَةٌ طَرَحْتُهُ عَنْ ظَهْرِ رَسُولِ اللَّهِ صلى الله عليه وسلم وَالنَّبِيُّ صلى الله عليه وسلم سَاجِدٌ مَا يَرْفَعُ رَأْسَهُ حَتَّى انْطَلَقَ إِنْسَانٌ فَأَخْبَرَ فَاطِمَةَ فَجَاءَتْ وَهِيَ جُوَيْرِيَةٌ فَطَرَحَتْهُ عَنْهُ . ثُمَّ أَقْبَلَتْ عَلَيْهِمْ تَشْتِمُهُمْ

The one most accursed among them grabbed the afterbirth and, when the Prophet ﷺ went down in prostration, he placed it between his shoulders. Then they laughed at him and some of them leaned upon the others with laughter. And I (Ibn Mas'ūd) stood looking. If I had the power, I would have thrown it away from the back of the Messenger of Allāh ﷺ. The Prophet ﷺ was prostrating and did not raise up until a man went to his house and informed (his daughter) Fātimah, who was a young girl at that time, about what happened. She came and removed it from him. Then, she turned toward them, rebuking them.

فَلَمَّا قَضَى النَّبِيُّ صلى الله عليه وسلم صَلاَتَهُ رَفَعَ صَوْتَهُ ثُمَّ دَعَا عَلَيْهِمْ وَكَانَ إِذَا دَعَا دَعَا ثَلاَثًا . وَإِذَا سَأَلَ سَأَلَ ثَلاَثًا ثُمَّ قَالَ " اللَّهُمَّ عَلَيْكَ بِقُرَيْشٍ". ثَلاَثَ مَرَّاتٍ فَلَمَّا سَمِعُوا صَوْتَهُ ذَهَبَ عَنْهُمُ الضِّحْكُ وَخَافُوا دَعْوَتَهُ

When the Prophet ﷺ had finished his prayer, he raised his voice and supplicated against them. When he would supplicate, he would repeat the du'ā three times, and when he asked (Allāh) for something, he asked thrice. Then he said three times, 'O Allāh, it is for You to deal with the Quraysh.' When they heard his voice, laughter vanished from them, and they feared his supplication.

ثُمَّ قَالَ " اللَّهُمَّ عَلَيْكَ بِأَبِي جَهْلِ بْنِ هِشَامٍ وَعُتْبَةَ بْنِ رَبِيعَةَ وَشَيْبَةَ بْنِ رَبِيعَةَ وَالْوَلِيدِ بْنِ عُقْبَةَ وَأُمَيَّةَ بْنِ خَلَفٍ وَعُقْبَةَ بْنِ أَبِي مُعَيْطٍ ". وَذَكَرَ السَّابِعَ وَلَمْ أَحْفَظْهُ

Then he said, 'O Allāh, it is for You to deal with Abū Jahl ibn Hishām, and 'Utba ibn Rabī'a, and Shaība ibn Rabī'a and Al-Walīd ibn 'Utbah[36], and Umāyyah ibn Khalaf, and 'Uqba ibn Abū Mu'aīt.' And he mentioned the name of the seventh person which I did not remember.

فَوَالَّذِي بَعَثَ مُحَمَّدًا صلى الله عليه وسلم بِالْحَقِّ لَقَدْ رَأَيْتُ الَّذِينَ سَمَّى صَرْعَى يَوْمَ بَدْرٍ ثُمَّ سُحِبُوا إِلَى الْقَلِيبِ قَلِيبِ بَدْرٍ

By One Who sent Muhammad with truth, I saw those he had named lying slain on the Day of Badr. Their dead bodies were dragged to be thrown into a well near the battlefield."[37]

[36] In *Sahīh Muslim* he is mentioned as Al-Walīd ibn 'Uqbah, but what is correct is he is Al-Walīd ibn 'Utbah.

[37] *Sahīh Muslim*, 1794.

In the narration collected by Ahmad it states, 'Abdullāh ibn Mas'ūd said, "I never saw the Messenger of Allāh ﷺ supplicate against the tribe of Quraysh except for one day. He was praying while a group of men from the Quraysh were sitting with the afterbirth of a she-camel nearby. They said, 'Who will throw the afterbirth on his back?' 'Uqba ibn Abū Mu'aīt said, 'I will!' So, he took the afterbirth and threw it on his back."

The remaining portion of this hadīth is like the previously mentioned hadīth. At the end of this narration, he said, "'Abdullāh ibn Mas'ūd said, 'I saw them slain on the Day of Badr. And they were tossed in a well except for Umāyyah because he was a huge man; thus, parts of his body were separated before he was thrown in the well.'"[38]

In the narration collected by Bukhārī, the Messenger of Allāh ﷺ said, "A curse descended upon the companions of the well."[39]

This hadīth was narrated by Abū Na'īm in the book *Evidence of Prophecy*, with a similar narration to the previously mentioned hadīth. He said, "After the Prophet ﷺ supplicated against them, he exited from the masjid and encountered Abū al-Bakhtarī, a pagan from the tribe of Quraysh. Abū al-Bakhtarī had his whip with him. He noticed the face of the Prophet ﷺ, so he took hold of him and asked what was wrong. The Prophet ﷺ said, 'Leave me be.' Abū al-Bakhtarī said, 'I implore you by Allāh ﷻ, I will not leave you until you tell me what happened, something has happened to you!' When the Prophet ﷺ realized that he was not going to leave him until he informed him of what happened. He said, 'Abū Jahl ordered his companions to toss the afterbirth of a she-camel on me.' Abū al-Bakhtarī said, 'Let's go to the masjid.' The Prophet ﷺ declined, but Abū al-Bakhtarī insisted. Abū al-Bakhtarī entered

---

[38] Sahīh al-Bukhari, 3185.

[39] *Sahīh al-Bukhārī*, 520.

the masjid, turned to Abū Jahl and said, 'O Abū al-Hakam,[40] are you the one who ordered them to toss camel afterbirth on Muhammad?' Abū Jahl said, 'Yes.' Abū al-Bakhtarī raised his whip and struck Abū Jahl in the head. The men present (some siding with Abū Jahl and others siding with Abū al-Bakhtarī) began to fight each other. Abū Jahl yelled, 'Woe to you! Muhammad only wants to place animosity between us, so he and his companions will be victorious.'"

The Three Main Antagonists of the Messenger of Allah

Ibn Sa'd narrated in his book *The Book of the Major Classifications* that Yaqūb ibn 'Utbah said, "The people of animosity toward the Prophet ﷺ and his companions (those who desired to dispute with him) were Abū Jahl ibn Hishām, and Abū Lahab ibn 'Abdul Muttalib." He went on to mention 20 men from the leaders of the disbelievers and chieftains of the Quraysh. Then he said, "All of the hatred and animosity returns back to three men, Abū Jahl ibn Hishām, Abū Lahab ibn 'Abdul Muttalib, and 'Uqba ibn Abū Mu'aīt."

Allāh ﷻ took revenge against the three of them and brought joy to His Prophet Muhammad ﷺ with their destruction.

---

[40] Translator's note: Abū al-Hakam, meaning the owner of wisdom, was the kunya he selected for himself. The Prophet ﷺ named him Abū Jahl, meaning the owner of ignorance.

THE STORY OF ABU JAHL

As for Abū Jahl, he was killed during the Battle of Badr. He was struck by the two sons of Afrā'.[41]

'Abdur-Rahmān bin Awf said, "While I was fighting in the front line on the day of Badr, suddenly I looked behind me and saw on my right and left two young boys and did not feel safe by standing between them. Then, one of them asked me secretly so that his companion may not hear, 'O Uncle! Show me Abū Jahl.' I said, 'O nephew! What will you do to him?' He said, 'I have promised Allāh that if I see him, I will either kill him or be killed before I kill him.' Then the other said the same to me secretly so that his companion should not hear. I would not have been pleased to be in between two other men instead of them. I pointed Abū Jahl out to them. Both of them attacked him like two hawks until they knocked him down. Those two boys were the sons of Afrā'."[42]

Al-Bayhaqī narrated in *Evidence of Prophecy*, "The Prophet ﷺ said, 'May Allāh have mercy upon the two sons of Afrā'. They shared in the killing of the Pharoah of this nation and the head of the leaders of disbelief.' It was said, 'O Messenger of Allāh, who killed him with them?' He said, 'The angels and Ibn Mas'ūd participated in killing him.'"[43]

Ibn Kathīr said in his book *Al-Bidāyah wa Nihāyah*, "The killing of Abū Jahl was at the hands of youth from the Ansār. After that, 'Abdullāh ibn Mas'ūd took hold of his beard and stood on his chest. Abū Jahl said to him, 'You have climbed high little shepherd.' After he took his last breath, 'Abdullāh ibn Mas'ūd took his head and placed it in front of the

[41] Afrā' is the name of their mother.

[42] Sahīh al-Bukhārī, 3988.

[43] Al-Bayhaqī, *Evidence of Prophecy*.

Messenger of Allāh ﷺ. Thus, Allāh ﷻ brought relief to the hearts of the believers. And this was far more beneficial to them than if Abū Jahl would have died from a lightning strike, or if his roof would have caved in on him, or if he would have died from natural causes."

Al-Bayhaqī narrated in *Evidence of Prophecy* that Ibn Ishāq said, "When the glad tidings came to the Messenger of Allāh ﷺ concerning the killing of Abū Jahl, and they swore by Allāh ﷻ three times that they had seen him slain, the Messenger of Allāh ﷺ fell down prostrate giving gratitude to Allāh." Al-Bayhaqī also narrated from 'Abdullāh ibn Abī Aufā that the Messenger of Allāh ﷺ prayed the Duhā prayer after the conquest of Mecca and when the head of Abū Jahl was brought to him.

As for Abū Lahab and 'Uqba ibn Abū Mu'aīt, both were neighbors of the Messenger of Allāh ﷺ and they used to severely harass him. 'Ā'ishah ﵂ said the Messenger of Allāh ﷺ said, "I was between two evil neighbors, Abū Jahl and 'Uqba ibn Abū Mu'aīt. They would bring animal intestines and throw them at my door."[44]

Shortly after the Battle of Badr, Allāh ﷻ eradicated Abū Lahab and united him with his brothers from the leaders of the disbelievers and chieftains of the Quraysh. This was after he received the news that the other leaders had been slain in the battle.

---

[44] Translator's note: Shaykh al-Albānī declared this narration as weak and fabricated in his collection of weak hadīth.

THE STORY OF ABU LAHAB

Abū Rāfi', the freed slave of the Messenger of Allāh ﷺ, was under the care of Al-'Abbās while in Mecca, and he concealed his Islām due to the oppression of the pagans. Abū Lahab stayed behind from the Battle of Badr. When Abū Sufyān returned from Badr, Abū Lahab asked him which side was victorious. Abū Sufyān replied, "They killed us however they wanted, and captured us however they wanted, but I do not blame our people." Abū Lahab said, "Why not?" Abū Sufyān said, "By Allāh, I saw men dressed in all white riding piebald horses and nothing could harm them!" Abū Rafi' said, "Upon hearing this I said, 'Those were angels!'" Thus, Abū Lahab slapped me across my face, threw me to the ground, stood over me and began to beat me until he was kneeling on my chest. Umm al-Fadl stood up, grabbed a tent pole, and struck Abū Lahab in the head, fracturing his skull. She said, "O enemy of Allāh, you think it is okay to attack him because his master is not here!'" Abū Lahab's wound became septic, and he died seven days later from an ulcer.

His sons left his body inside his home for two or three nights until his body began to decay. A man from the Quraysh said, "Are you not ashamed to leave the decaying body of your father in his home?" They replied, "We are afraid of the ulcer." So they sent in slaves to remove his body. It was hosed with water, from a distance, then pushed with poles into a grave outside Mecca, and stones were thrown over it.[45]

---

[45] Collected by Al-Hakim, 5415 and At-Tabarānī, 907.

The Story of 'Uqba ibn Abu Mu'ait

Ibn al-Athīr mentioned in his book *The Complete History*, "'Uqba ibn Abū Mu'aīt was from the most severe antagonists of the Messenger of Allāh ﷺ and the Muslims. 'Uqba would take entrails and place them at the door of the Messenger of Allāh ﷺ. One day, Tulayb ibn Umayr, the cousin of the Prophet ﷺ, saw 'Uqba placing entrails at the door of the Prophet ﷺ. The mother of Tulayb was Arwā bint 'Abdul Muttalib, the paternal aunt of the Messenger of Allāh ﷺ. Tulayb picked up the entrails, threw them on the head of 'Uqba and grabbed him by the ears. 'Uqba went to Arwā, the mother of Tulayb, to complain about her son. He said, 'Your son has begun protecting Muhammad!' She said, 'And who is more deserving to protect him than us? And who is more deserving of our wealth and our lives other than Muhammad?'"[46]

'Uqba was captured at the Battle of Badr. 'Āsim ibn Thābit al-Ansārī ؓ was tasked with executing 'Uqba. When 'Uqba was about to be killed, he said, "O Muhammad, who will look after my children?" He responded, "The Hellfire."[47]

'Uqba said, "Will you kill me, O Muhammad, in front of the Quraysh?" The Messenger of Allāh ﷺ said, "Yes. Do you all know what he did to me? He came behind me while I was prostrating and placed his foot on my neck. He pressed his foot down and did not raise it until he thought my eyes had left the socket. He came another time and threw the intes-

---

[46] Collected by Ibn Sa'd, 124.

[47] Sunan Abī Dāwūd, 2686.

tines of a she-camel on my head while I was prostrating. Thus, Fātimah came and washed it away from my head."[48]

THE STORY OF UMM JAMIL, THE WIFE OF ABU LAHAB

From the stories of those who harmed the Messenger of Allāh ﷺ is the story of Umm Jamīl, the wife of Abū Lahab. Al-Balādhurī said, "Umm Jamīl bint Harb used to harm the Messenger of Allāh ﷺ a great deal. She is the carrier of the firewood. Allāh named her this because she would carry thorns during the night and throw them on the path the Prophet ﷺ and his companions would walk on in order to injure them. One day, she was carrying a tied bundle of thorns and sat down on a stone to rest when an angel came from behind her, pulled the rope she had around her neck, and choked her with it."[49]

THE STORY OF 'UTBAH, THE SON OF ABU JAHL

From the stories of those who harmed the Messenger of Allāh ﷺ is the story of 'Utbah, the son of Abū Jahl. Ruqayah, the daughter of the Messenger of Allāh ﷺ, married 'Utbah ibn Abī Lahab and Umm Kulthūm, the daughter of the Messenger of Allāh ﷺ, married 'Utaybah

[48] Ibn Kathīr, *Al-Bidāyah wa Nihāyah.*

[49] Al-Bayhaqī, *Evidence of Prophecy*, page 319.

ibn Abī Lahab. While they were married, the following verse was revealed:

﴿ تَبَّتْ يَدَا أَبِي لَهَبٍ وَتَبَّ ۝١ ﴾

Perish the two hands of Abū Lahab and perish he![50]

When this verse was revealed, 'Utbah's father, Abū Lahab said, "My head is impermissible for your head (meaning I will not speak to you) if you do not divorce his daughter." Thus, 'Utbah divorced Ruqayah before the marriage was consummated, and 'Utaybah divorced Umm Kulthūm before the marriage was consummated.

Mu'āwiya ibn Muslim narrated that his father said, "Abū Lahab and his son used to insult the Prophet ﷺ and supplicate against him. The Prophet ﷺ said:

اللَّهُمَّ سَلِّطِ عَلَيْهِ كلبًا مِنْ كِلَابِكَ

O Allāh, set loose against him a dog from your dogs.

Abū Lahab was sending some of his merchandise to Shām. He sent his son along with his servants to deliver the product. He said to them, "I fear for my son due to the supplication of Muhammad, so watch over him." When they would rest for the night during their travel to Shām, they would place 'Utbah next to a wall and put clothing over him to hide him. Habbār ibn al-Aswad,[51] who was sent to watch over 'Utbah, said, 'I saw a lion sniffing each of us, one by one, until it found 'Utbah

---

[50] Surah al-Masad, 111:1.

[51] Translator's note: Habbār ibn al-Aswad was a pagan at this time, but he eventually went to the Prophet ﷺ and embraced Islām.

and snatched him.' When this news reached Abū Lahab, he said, 'Did not I tell you that I feared the supplication of Muhammad!'"[52]

THE STORY OF ʻUBAY IBN KHALAF

From the stories of those who harmed the Messenger of Allāh ﷺ is the story of Ubay ibn Khalaf. Saʻīd ibn al-Musayyib narrated,[54] "Ubay ibn Khalaf was captured during the Battle of Badr. When he purchased his freedom from the Messenger of Allāh ﷺ, he said to the Messenger of Allāh ﷺ, 'Indeed I have a stallion that I feed a bushel of corn every day, so perhaps I can kill you while riding him!' The Messenger of Allāh ﷺ said, 'On the contrary, I will kill you while you are on it, insha'Allāh.' During the Battle of Uhud, Ubay rode toward the Prophet ﷺ on that stallion. When he got close, some men from the Muslims went forward to kill him. The Messenger of Allāh ﷺ said to them, 'Stay back, stay back.' Then, he stood and threw his spear, scrapping the back of Ubay's neck. Ubay went to his companions and fell down. They said to him, 'There is nothing wrong with you, it is just a little scrape.' Ubay replied, 'Did he not say he was going to kill me, insha'Allāh. If this would have happened to the tribe of Dhu al-Majāz, they would have all died!' Ubay died on his way home. This is the only person the Prophet ﷺ killed with his own hand."

[52] Al-Bayhaqī, *Evidence of Prophecy*. Al-Hakim said the chain of narration is authentic.
[54] Collected by ibn Saʻd in *The Book of the Major Classifications*.

The Story of Nawfal ibn Khuwaylid

Nawfal ibn Khuwaylid was from those who caused great harm to the Messenger of Allāh ﷺ and the Muslims. He was the half-brother of Khadījah ؓ, the wife of the Prophet ﷺ. On the Day of Badr, the Messenger of Allāh ﷺ said, "O Allāh, suffice me on Nawfal ibn Khuwaylid." After the battle, the Messenger of Allāh ﷺ said, "Who has information concerning Nawfal ibn Khuwaylid?" 'Ālī ibn Abī Tālib ؓ said, "I killed him." The Prophet ﷺ exalted Allāh and said, "All praises belong to Allāh, the One who answered my supplication."[55]

The Story of Nadr ibn al-Harith

From the stories of those who harmed the Messenger of Allāh ﷺ is the story of Nadr ibn al-Hārith. Nadr was from the devils of the Quraysh. He used to harass the Messenger of Allāh ﷺ and display great animosity toward him.[56] Ibn Athīr said,[58] "Nadr was the most antagonistic from the tribe of Quraysh against the Prophet ﷺ, and would harm him and his companions. Before the Prophet ﷺ received revelation, Nadr used to read the books of the Persians and interact with the Jews and Christians, and he was expecting the appearance of the Prophet ﷺ. If a warner came to them, he would say they would be more guided than any of the nations before them. Allāh ﷻ sent down the verse about him:

[55] Al-Bayhaqī, *Evidence of Prophecy.*

[56] Al-Bayhaqī, *Evidence of Prophecy.*

[58] *The Complete History.*

﴿ وَأَقْسَمُوا بِاللَّهِ جَهْدَ أَيْمَانِهِمْ لَئِن جَاءَهُمْ نَذِيرٌ لَّيَكُونُنَّ أَهْدَىٰ مِنْ إِحْدَى الْأُمَمِ ۖ فَلَمَّا جَاءَهُمْ نَذِيرٌ مَّا زَادَهُمْ إِلَّا نُفُورًا ﴿٤٢﴾ ﴾

And they swore by Allāh ﷻ their most binding oath, that if a warner came to them, they would be more guided than any of the nations (before them), yet when a warner (Muhammad) came to them, it increased in them nothing but flight (from the truth).[59]

Nadr would say, "Muhammad is only telling tales of the ancients." Several verses were sent down about him. Miqdād captured him during the Battle of Badr and the Messenger of Allāh ﷺ ordered him to be executed. Thus, 'Ālī ibn Abī Tālib cut his neck.

THE STORY OF 'AMIR IBN TUFAYL AND ARBAD IBN QAYS

Two major enemies of the Messenger of Allāh ﷺ were 'Āmir ibn Tufayl and Arbad ibn Qays. Ibn Ishāq said, "A delegation from Banī 'Āmir came to see the Messenger of Allāh ﷺ and among them were 'Āmir ibn Tufayl, Arbad ibn Qays, and Jabbār ibn Sulmā. These three were the leaders of their people and their devils.[60] 'Āmir ibn Tufayl, the enemy of Allāh ﷻ,[61] approached the Messenger of Allāh ﷺ with a plan to assassinate him. His tribe said to him, 'O 'Āmir, the people have embraced

[59] Surah Fātir, 35:42.

[60] Translator's note: Jabbār ibn Sulmā would eventually embrace Islām ؓ.

[61] Translator's note: 'Āmir ibn Tufayl ordered the killing of 70 Qur'ān reciters, sent to invite his people to Islām.

Islām; thus, you need to embrace Islām also.' 'Āmir said, 'By Allāh, I swore that I would never stop until the Arabs followed my footsteps, now should I follow this youth?!'

Then 'Āmir said to Arbad, 'When we approach this man (meaning the Messenger of Allāh ﷺ) I will distract him, then you can strike him with the sword.' When they approached him, 'Āmir said to the Messenger of Allāh ﷺ, 'Speak to me privately.' The Prophet ﷺ said, 'No, by Allāh, not until you believe in Allāh, alone.' 'Āmir said, 'O Muhammad, speak to me in private.' As he was speaking to him, he was looking to see if Arbad was going to proceed and attack the Prophet ﷺ, but Arbad did not do anything. When he saw Arbad was not moving, he said, 'O Muhammad, speak to me privately.' The Prophet ﷺ said, 'Not until you believe in Allāh, alone, without partners.'

'Āmir said, 'O Muhammad, what will I get if I embrace Islām?' The Prophet ﷺ said, 'You will receive what the other Muslims receive, and you will have the same responsibilities.' 'Āmir said, 'Will you place me as the leader of the Muslims after you die?' The Prophet ﷺ said, 'No, this position is not for you or your people.' 'Āmir said, 'Are you offering me a rabbit while you have the towns and its people!' The Prophet ﷺ responded, 'No, I will give you free rein over the horses.' 'Āmir said, 'I already have horses.'

When 'Āmir saw the Prophet ﷺ was not going to agree, he said, 'By Allāh, I will bring horses and men against you!' When he turned away, the Messenger of Allāh ﷺ said, 'O Allāh, suffice me against 'Āmir ibn Tufayl.'

When they left, the Messenger of Allāh ﷺ, 'Āmir said to Arbad, 'Woe to you, why did you not do what I commanded you to do? By Allāh, there was not a man on the face of earth whom I feared more than you, but I will not fear you after today.' Arbad said, 'Do not blame me. By Allāh, I was prepared to do what you commanded me to do, but you were standing between me and him so I could only see you. Did you want me to hit you with the sword?'

They left, returning to their land, and while on the road, Allāh ﷻ sent a disease that infects young camels to 'Āmir ibn Tufayl. His companions carried him to the home of a woman from the tribe of Banī Salūl. As he was dying, he began shouting, "O tribe of Banī 'Āmir, I have the same disease that kills camels, and I'm dying in the home of a woman from Banī Salūl!' (The tribe of Banī 'Āmir viewed the Banī Salūl as a lowly tribe.)

When his companions returned his corpse to the land of Banī 'Āmir, the people asked Arbad what occurred. Arbad said, 'He invited us to worship something. I wish he was here now so I could shoot him with an arrow and kill him.' A day or two after saying this, Arbad was riding a camel of his, intending to sell it. Allāh ﷻ sent a lightning bolt, killing him and the camel. Arbad was the maternal brother of the Companion Labīd ibn Rabī'ah.

Ibn Hishām narrated that Ibn 'Abbās said that Allāh ﷻ sent down verses in the Qur'ān concerning them. Allāh ﷻ said:

﴿ وَيُسَبِّحُ الرَّعْدُ بِحَمْدِهِ وَالْمَلَائِكَةُ مِنْ خِيفَتِهِ وَيُرْسِلُ الصَّوَاعِقَ فَيُصِيبُ بِهَا مَن يَشَاءُ وَهُمْ يُجَادِلُونَ فِي اللَّهِ وَهُوَ شَدِيدُ الْمِحَالِ ﴿١٣﴾ ﴾

And ar-Ra'd (thunder) glorifies and praises Him, and so do the angels because of His Awe, He sends the thunderbolts, and therewith He strikes whom He wills,

yet they (disbelievers) dispute about Allāh. And He is Mighty in strength and Severe in punishment.[62]

THE ROMAN WHO INTENDED TO DISRESPECT THE GRAVE OF THE PROPHET

From the stories of quick retaliation is what has been narrated by 'Ālī ibn Ahmad al-Samhūdī in his book *Wafa al-Wafa bi Akhbar Dar al-Mustafa*. Ibn Zabāla[63] said, "More than one scholar has mentioned the following story to me. There was an expansion of the Prophet's Masjid during the era of al-Walīd ibn 'Abdul Mālik. Al-Walīd wrote a letter to the king of Rome, saying, 'We intend to expand the masjid of our greatest Prophet, so send some workers to assist us.' The king of Rome sent around 20 workers. During the day, as the workers worked in the masjid, they found the masjid was empty. One of them said, 'Should I urinate on their Prophet?' As he prepared to urinate on the Prophet's grave, his companions prevented him from doing so. As he started again to do it, he flipped upside down, landing on his head and his brain spilled out. Some of the Christian workers present immediately embraced Islām.

[62] Surah ar-Ra'd, 13:13.

[63] Translator's note: Muhammad ibn Hassan ibn Zabāla died 199 AH.

THE ARROGANT MAN WHO DENIED THE EXISTENCE OF ALLAH

Ibn Jarīr[64] ﵀ narrated from 'Ālī ibn Abī Tālib ﵁ that he said,[66] "A man came to the Prophet ﷺ and said, 'O Muhammad, tell me about the One you are calling to. Is He made of pearls or is He made of gold?' Thus, Allāh ﷻ sent down a lightning strike, scorching him. Then, the verse was sent down:

﴿ وَيُرْسِلُ الصَّوَاعِقَ فَيُصِيبُ بِهَا مَن يَشَاءُ وَهُمْ يُجَادِلُونَ فِي اللَّهِ وَهُوَ شَدِيدُ الْمِحَالِ ﴿١٣﴾ ﴾

He sends the thunderbolts, and therewith He strikes whom He wills, yet they (disbelievers) dispute about Allāh. And He is Mighty in strength and Severe in punishment.[67]

THE MAN WHO RIDICULED THE MISWAK

This is the story of the ignorant, reckless man who ridiculed the Sunnah. This story was mentioned by Ibn Khallikān[68] and it was also men-

---

64 Translator's note: Muhammad ibn Jarīr al-Tabari is the noble scholar of *tafsīr*. He died 310 AH.

66 *Tafsīr at-Tabari*, Sūrah ar-Ra'd, 13:13.

67 Sūrah ar-Ra'd. 13:13.

68 Translator's note: He is the Muslim historian, Ahmad bin Muhammad. He died 681 AH.

tioned by Shaykh Qutb ad-Dīn al-Yūnīnī.[69] He said, "It has reached us that a man named Abū Salamah from Egypt was known to be ignorant and reckless. One day the miswak toothbrush was mentioned to him and the virtues of it. He responded by saying, 'By Allāh, I would only use the miswak in my anus.' Then he took a miswak, placed it in his rectum, and removed it. Nine months later he began to complain about abdominal pains, then his stomach expanded like a pregnant woman. An animal exited from his body that resembled a rat, with a head like a fish. It had four protruding teeth, four limbs, and a rear end resembling a rabbit. When the creature exited him, it screamed three times. The man's daughter entered the room and hit the creature on the head, killing it. Three days later, the man died while saying, 'This creature destroyed my internal organs.' A group of people and the khatīb of that area witnessed this creature. This occurred in the year 655 AH, and the story was mentioned by Ibn Kathīr in *Al-Bidāyah wa Nihāyah*. It was also mentioned by Ibn al-'Imād al-Hanbalī.

This story is a lesson for those who take heed and an admonition for those who ridiculed the authentic hadīth from the Prophet ﷺ. They reject the hadīth in the vilest manner without giving it any concern, especially the narrations that oppose their limited intellects and corrupt opinions. We have seen this in the books and statements of some of the boorish individuals who are amazed with themselves and their faulty writings. Their numbers are prevalent during our current era. I ask Allāh ﷻ not to increase their numbers.

---

[69] Translator's note: He is the Muslim historian and scholar of hadīth. He died 726 AH.

The Man Who Belied the Decree of Allah

From these stories is the story of the man who belied the decree of Allāh ﷻ. This story was collected by Imām al-Lalikā'ī[70] *in Explanation of the Sunnah* from Hamād ibn Zayd. He said, "A man made a wager with another man that he could swim across the river. He swam until he was close to the shore. He said, 'I have crossed the river.' The other man said to him, 'Say insha'Allāh.' The man responded, 'Whether He wills or not!' So earth seized him."

Those Who Insulted Abu Bakr and 'Umar

From the stories of those who insulted the Companions, is what has been mentioned by Ibn al-Qayyim in his book *The Soul*. One of the Salaf said, "I had a neighbor who used to insult Abū Bakr and 'Umar ﷺ. One day, he insulted them more than he had done previously, so I criticized him and he criticized me. Then we departed from one another while I was upset and sad. I went to bed that night without eating dinner. I saw the Messenger of Allāh ﷺ in a dream that night. I said, 'O Messenger of Allāh, so-and-so insults your companions.' He said, 'Which companions?' I said, 'Abū Bakr and 'Umar.' He said, 'Take this blade and slaughter him with it.' So I took the blade, placed it on his neck, and slaughtered him. The blood flowed down my hand. I tossed the blade and he fell down in front of me. I was awakened from my

---

[70] Translator's note: He is the noble scholar Hibat Allāh ibn al-Hasan. He died 418 years after the migration.

dream when I heard a scream coming from the direction of his house. I went out and asked, 'What happened!?' They said, 'So-and-so died suddenly!' When the sun rose, we went to see him, and he had a line on his neck in the place he was cut in my dream." This story was mentioned by Ibn al-Jawzī in the biography of 'Umar ibn al-Khattab.

Also from the stories of those who insulted the Companions is what was mentioned from Ibn al-Qayyim in his book *The Soul*, narrated from Al-Qayrawani.[71] Muhammad ibn 'Abdullāh al-Mahbali said, "I saw in a dream as though I was on an open plain belonging to so-and-so. Suddenly, I saw the Prophet ﷺ sitting on a mound of dirt along with Abū Bakr, while 'Umar was standing in front of them. 'Umar ؓ said to him, 'O Messenger of Allāh, this person insulted me, and he insulted Abū Bakr.' He said, 'Bring him to me, O Abū Hafs.' 'Umar brought a man from Omān, and he was known from insulting Abū Bakr and 'Umar. The Prophet ﷺ said, 'Lie him on his side.' So he laid him on his side and slaughtered him. I was awakened by a loud scream. I said to myself, 'I should go advise him perchance he may repent.' When I got close to his home, I heard loud crying. I said, 'What is the crying about?' They said, 'The Omāni man was slaughtered last night on his bed.' I went close to him and saw a line on his neck from ear to ear which looked like trapped blood."

From the stories of those who insulted the Companions, is what has been narrated by Imām al-Lalikā'ī in his book *The Explanation of the Sunnah*. Ummār ibn Sayf ad-Dabī said, "We went out for a battle on the sea under the command of Mūsā ibn Ka'b al-Tamīmī. There was a man on the ship with us called Abū Himmān. He began insulting Abū Bakr and 'Umar, and we warned him but he did not take heed. We admon-

---

[71] Translator's note: He is Ibn Abī Zayd al-Qayrawani. He died in the year 386 AH.

ished him but he did not stop. When we reached an island, we disembarked and separated so everyone could perform *wudhū* for Dhuhr prayer. We were informed that hornets attacked Abū Himān. When we looked for him, we found the hornets had killed him." Najdah ibn al-Mubārak added, "Some people attempted to bury him, but the ground became rough and hard, so they were unable to dig a hole. Thus, we threw a rock and some leaves on him."

Al-Khatīb al-Baghdadi narrated in his book *The History of Baghdad*, from Ismael ibn Hamād ibn Abī Hanīfah, he said, "We had a neighbor who was a Rāfidah. He had two mules. He named one of them Abū Bakr and the other 'Umar. One night, one of the mules attacked him and killed him. Abū Hanīfah was informed of this, and he replied, 'Look to see if the mule that killed him was the mule he named Umar.' So we looked and that was the case. The mule the Rāfidah named 'Umar had killed him."

THE DOG AND SUFYAN AT-THAWRI

Imām al-Lalikā'ī stated in his book *The Explanation of the Sunnah* that Sufyān at-Thawrī said, "I went out to the masjid during the last third of the night. Our neighbor had a ravenous dog, so I sat watching it, waiting for it to step aside. The dog said to me, 'Pass by, O Abū 'Abdullāh, for I have only been commanded to attack those who insult Abū Bakr and 'Umar.'"

Those Who Insulted Ali

Al-Hākim narrated that Qays ibn Abī Hāzim[72] said, "I was in Madinah walking around the markets when I reached the place known as the Oil Stones.[73] I saw a group of people gathering around a knight riding on his horse while he was slandering 'Ālī ibn Abī Tālib. The people were standing around him when Sa'd ibn Abī Waqās arrived and said, 'What is this about?' They said, 'This man is insulting 'Ālī ibn Abī Tālib.' The group split so Sa'd could stand in front of him. Sa'd said to him, 'Why are you insulting 'Ālī ibn Abī Tālib? Was he not the first man to embrace Islām? Was he not the first person to pray with the Messenger of Allāh ﷺ? Was he not the person that abstained from the worldly life the most? Was he not from the most knowledgeable of people? Didn't the Messenger of Allāh ﷺ make him his son-in-law by marrying him to his daughter? Did he not carry the flag of the Messenger of Allāh ﷺ in his wars?' Then Sa'd turned and faced the Qibla, raised his hands and said, 'O Allāh, this person insulted Your ally; thus, do not allow this gathering to disperse until You show them Your power.' Qays said, 'I swear by Allāh, the crowd did not disperse until his animal slipped, throwing him such that he landed on his head, causing his skull to crack and his brain spilled out and he died.'" Al-Hākim said, "This narration is authentic based upon the conditions of Bukhārī and Muslim."

From the stories of those who insulted the Companions is that which has been collected by al-Hākim in his book *Al-Mustadrak*, from Mus'ab ibn Sa'd concerning Sa'd ibn Abī Waqās ﷺ. He said, "A man insulted

---

[72] Translator's note: He is Qays ibn Abī Hāzim, the noble scholar from the second generation. He died 98 AH.

[73] Translator's note: The Oil Stones is the place where the Prophet ﷺ would go out to pray for rain.

'Ālī ﷺ, so Sa'd supplicated against the man. After his supplication, a camel came toward the man and killed him. Afterwards, Sa'd freed a slave and vowed to never supplicate against anyone again."

The Man Who Insulted Abu Hurairah

From the stories of those who insulted the Companions is what was mentioned by Abū Sa'd al-Sam'ānī from Al-Qādir Abū Tayyib Tabarī. He said, "We were sitting in a masjid in Bagdad when an Iranian came and asked us about buying a goat with its udder tied. We answered him and used as a proof the hadīth of Abū Hurairah ﷺ. The man began to insult Abū Hurairah, when suddenly a snake fell from the ceiling and moved across the floor until it entered the circle. It went directly to the Iranian man and attacked him, killing him." Shaykh al-Islām Ibn Taymiyyah mentioned this story in his answer in refutation of those who insult Abū Hurairah ﷺ. This answer is in the fourth volume in his collection of religious verdicts, pages 532 to 539. Thus, go back and review the speech of the Shaykh. For indeed, it is extremely important. Review the entire volume concerning his refutation on those who insult and belittle the Companions.

Those Who Attempted to Remove Abu Bakr and 'Umar from Their Graves

From the stories that serve as a warning, admonition, and lesson for the pious is that which was mentioned by Nūr al-Dīn al-Samhūdī in his book *Wafā' al-Wafā' bi Akhbar Dar al-Mustafa*. It was also mentioned by Muhibb al-Dīn Tabarī in his book *The Virtue of the Ten Promised Paradise*. He said, "It was mentioned by Harūn, the son of Shaykh 'Umar ibn az-Za'ab—and he is reliable, truthful, and known for his uprightness and worship—that he narrated from his father that he said, 'I was living next to Madinah. The Shaykh who was the custodian of the Prophet's Masjid was Shamsi Dīn Sawāb al-Lamtī. He was a righteous man who used to take care of the poor. He and I had a close relationship. One day he said to me, 'I will tell you something amazing.' I had a companion that would sit with the governor and inform me of information I needed to know. So, this day he came to me said, 'Something amazing happened today!' I asked what it was. He said, 'The Rāfidah of Aleppo (Syria) arrived and spent a long time with the governor. They requested he allow them to open the room of the Prophet ﷺ so they could remove Abū Bakr and 'Umar from their graves. They presented him with large sums of money and gifts, and the governor agreed to this. This caused me a great deal of stress and concern. The messenger of the governor came to me and said, 'O Sawāb, tonight some people will come to you at the masjid. Open the door for them and allow them to do what they want, and do not oppose them.' I responded, 'I hear and obey.' I left and spent the day behind the room crying until I had no more tears, and no one knew why I was crying. When the night arrived, I prayed the 'Ishā prayer. Everyone left the masjid and I locked the doors. That night, there was a knock on the door where the governor enters the masjid, meaning the door known as the Door of Salām. I opened the door and there were 40 men. I counted them one by one. They had with them their surveying tools, candles, and tools for demolition and digging.

They headed toward the room, and I swear by Allāh ﷻ they did not reach the minbar before the earth had swallowed all of them, collectively, along with their tools. No trace of them remained at all. The governor worried why information concerning them was slow to reach him, so he summoned for me and said, 'O Sawāb, did the people not come?' I said, 'Of course, and I allowed them in, but the earth opened and swallowed them.' The governor said, 'If you tell anyone about this, I will kill you!' Thus, I remained silent about this for as long as the governor remained alive.'"

The Couple Who Fornicated on the Day of ʿArafah

From the stories containing punishments, lessons and admonitions is what was mentioned by Shaykh Kamal ad-Dīn al-Idfawī in his book *At-Tāliʿ as-Saʿīd*. He said, "A man fornicated with a woman on the Day of ʿArafah and they became stuck together. They were carried away stuck together and they died in this state."

The Woman Who Lied on Saʿīd ibn Zayd

The story of Arwā bin Uwais, who lied on Saʿīd ibn Zayd, has been collected in Sahīh Muslim. Arwā bint Uwais claimed Saʿīd ibn Zayd oppressed her and took some of her land and her drinking well. Saʿīd said to her, "Leave this and remove your claim. For indeed, I heard the Messenger of Allāh ﷺ say:

مَنْ أَخَذَ شِبْرًا مِنَ الأَرْضِ بِغَيْرِ حَقِّهِ طُوِّقَهُ فِي سَبْعِ أَرَضِينَ يَوْمَ الْقِيَامَةِ

Whoever took a span of land without right will be made to wear around his neck seven earths on the Day of Resurrection.

She refused to remove her claim, so Sa'īd said, "O Allāh, if she is lying, take away her eyesight and make her grave in this drinking well." So, I saw her blind, stumbling around the wall, saying, 'The curse of Sa'īd has afflicted me.' As she was walking, she fell into the well and died, and this became her grave.[74]

AL-HAJJAJ IBN YUSUF'S KILLING OF SA'ID IBN JUBAYR

From the punishments upon those who killed the righteous people is what occurred to Al-Hajjaj ibn Yūsūf due to his killing of Sa'īd ibn Jubayr. His story was mentioned by Abū al-Arab Muhammad ibn Ahmad ibn Tamām al-Tamīmī in his book *Al-Mihan*. It is a long story with several chains of transmission. Sa'īd ibn Jubayr supplicated against Al-Hajjaj before he slaughtered him. He said, "O Allāh, do not grant him power to kill anyone after me." Thus, Al-Hajjaj did not kill anyone after him. Sixteen days later, he developed an ulcer in his stomach, so he called for a doctor to examine him. The doctor took a piece of rotten meat, tied it to a black string, and placed it down his throat for an hour. When he removed the meat there were worms attached to the meat. Therefore, the doctor knew Al-Hajjaj was not going to survive. Each time Al-Hajjaj attempted to sleep, he would see Sa'īd ibn Jubayr in a dream, pulling his garment saying to him, "O enemy of Allāh, why did

[74] Sahīh Muslim, 1610.

you kill me?!" Al-Hajjaj was informed that Sa'īd ibn Jubayr supplicated against him that he would be afflicted with extreme cold. Those with him would place a furnace with hot coals around him to warm him. The coals were so hot they burned his clothes. But he continued to scream out due to the severity of the cold.

He called for Hassan al-Basrī to complain about his condition and apologize for what he had done. Hassan said to him, "I admonished you again and again to not harm the righteous and only treat them kindly, but you refused. If you would have left Sa'īd alone, Allāh would have left you alone. Therefore, what Allāh has decreed has come to pass and the book of your life span has come to an end." Afterwards Al-Hajjaj died.

What happened to Al-Hajjaj due to his killing Sa'īd ibn Jubayr is the severest warning and lesson to those who take heed. Therefore, take heed, those who harm and oppress the allies of Allāh ﷻ, know that Allāh is observing you. Take heed of the statement of Allāh ﷻ:

﴿ وَلَا تَحْسَبَنَّ اللَّهَ غَافِلًا عَمَّا يَعْمَلُ الظَّالِمُونَ إِنَّمَا يُؤَخِّرُهُمْ لِيَوْمٍ تَشْخَصُ فِيهِ الْأَبْصَارُ . مُهْطِعِينَ مُقْنِعِي رُءُوسِهِمْ لَا يَرْتَدُّ إِلَيْهِمْ طَرْفُهُمْ وَأَفْئِدَتُهُمْ هَوَاءٌ ﴾

And never think that Allāh is unaware of what the wrongdoers do. He only delays them for a Day when eyes will stare [in horror]. Racing ahead, their heads raised up, their glance does not come back to them, and their hearts are void.[75]

Also take heed of the statement of the Prophet ﷺ:

إِنَّ اللَّهَ لَيُمْلِي لِلظَّالِمِ حَتَّى إِذَا أَخَذَهُ لَمْ يُفْلِتْهُ

[75] Sūrah Ibrāhīm, 14:42-43.

Allāh gives respite to the oppressor, but when He takes hold of him, He never releases him.[76]

The Messenger of Allāh ﷺ said, "Allāh ﷻ said:

مَنْ عَادَى لِي وَلِيًّا فَقَدْ آذَنْتهُ بِالْحَرْبِ

Whosoever shows enmity to a friend of Mine, then I have declared war against him.[77]

'Ā'isha ﵂ said the Messenger of Allāh ﷺ said, that Allāh ﷻ said:

من أذلّ لي ولياً فقد استحل محاربتي

Whoever humiliates an ally of Mine, then indeed I have permitted my war against him.[78]

Therefore, let those who show animosity toward the allies of Allāh ﷻ take heed of these narrations, and prepare yourself for war with Allāh ﷻ if you have the ability to war with Him!

---

[76] Sahih al-Bukhārī, 4686.

[77] *40 Hadīth an-Nawawī*, Hadīth 38.

[78] Collected by Ahmad from the hadīth of 'Ā'isha.

Amir 'Abdul Aziz bin Mutaib al-Rashid's Killing of the Poor and Weak

From the punishment in this world for those who kill the poor and weak, those who have not committed any crimes, is what occurred with Amīr 'Abdul 'Azīz bin Muta'ib al-Rashīd.[79] That Amīr passed by Rawdah, a known village in the city of Qasim. There, he found 40 men who collected and sold herbage, and used the money to buy food and clothing for their families. The Amīr wanted to take revenge against the people of Qasim by killing these weak, poor men. Thus, he lined them all against the mountain and executed them. What a terrible and horrible catastrophe this was. Among those killed was an elderly man. His back was hunched over due to his old age. With him was a young, ten-year-old boy. The elderly man said to the Amīr, "Kill me, but leave this young boy because we have women at home with no one to take care of them after we are gone." The response of the Amīr was that he ordered the young boy to be executed first, while his father watched. The elderly man laughed. The Amīr said, "What has made you laugh?" The elderly man said, "I am laughing at Allāh's forbearance with you." So, he killed him and joined him with his son.

After this incident, the Amīr was not able to sleep. Each time he tried to sleep, he would see the elderly man choking him while saying, "O oppressor, by Allāh, you will not succeed!" This caused him tremendous terror. He would often awaken from sleep screaming, "What does this old man want with me?!" Not long after his horrible crime, he was killed in the village of Rawdah, the same place where he executed those

---

[79] Translator's note: 'Abdul 'Azīz bin Muta'ib al-Rashīd was the leader of the Emirate of Ha'īl or the Rashidi Emirate in Northern Arabian from 1897 to 1906.

poor people who collected the herbage. His head was severed and his body was transported to Buraydah, the capital of Qasim. This was a fitting punishment for him.

﴿ وَسَيَعْلَمُ الَّذِينَ ظَلَمُوا أَيَّ مُنقَلَبٍ يَنقَلِبُونَ ﴾

And those who do wrong will come to know by what overturning they will be overturned.[80]

Ibn 'Ajīl, a leader from the tribe of Shammar, attempted to advise him against killing these poor people collecting the herbage. He said to the Amīr, "Do not kill these weak people. By Allāh, the One Whom there is no deity worthy of worship except Him, if you kill them, the angels will war against you!" The Amīr responded by saying, "If I leave them, they will join their people and fight against me."

I say this heinous act is one of the evilest predicaments that have unfortunate consequences, as it is mentioned in the hadīth collected in Al-Bukhārī. 'Abdullāh ibn 'Umar ﷺ said:

إِنَّ مِنْ وَرْطَاتِ الأُمُورِ الَّتِي لاَ مَخْرَجَ لِمَنْ أَوْقَعَ نَفْسَهُ فِيهَا، سَفْكَ الدَّمِ الْحَرَامِ بِغَيْرِ حِلِّهِ.

One of the evil predicaments with bad consequence from which there is no escape for the one who is involved in it is to kill someone unlawfully.[81]

Al-Hafidh ibn Hajr said in his explanation to this narration, "The meaning of 'predicaments' is destruction, meaning that destruction from which there is not safety."

---

[80] Sūrah ash-Shu'arā, 26:227.

[81] Sahīh al-Bukhārī, 6863.

Innovators Who Slandered the People of Sunnah

From the punishments inflicted upon the people of innovation, those who show animosity toward the Sunnah and its people, is that which afflicted Ahmad ibn Abī Du'ād, Muhammad ibn 'Abdul Mālik al-Zayāt, and Harthama ibn A'yan due to their statement against Ahmad ibn Nasr. They said, "Indeed, Ahmad ibn Nasr al-Khazā'i was killed and died a disbeliever." And they invoked punishment upon themselves if this was not the case. Al-Khatīb al-Bagdadi mentioned their story in *The History of Bagdad.*

'Abdul 'Azīz ibn Yahyā al-Kinānī[82], the author of the book *Hayda*, said to Al-Mutawakkil,[84] "O leader of the believers, the most amazing thing seen is that Al-Wāthiq[85] killed Ahmad ibn Nasr and yet his tongue continued to recite the Qur'ān until he was buried in the ground!" Al-Mutawakkil became alarmed due to hearing this and became afraid for his brother, Al-Wāthiq, due to his killing of Ahmad ibn Nasr. When his minister, Muhammad ibn 'Abdul Mālik al-Zayyāt, entered upon him, Al-Mutawakkil expressed he was troubled due to the killing of Ahmad ibn Nasr. Muhammad ibn 'Abdul Mālik al-Zayyāt said, "O leader of the believers, may Allāh burn me with fire if the leader, Al-Wāthiq killed him while he was anything other than a disbeliever." Harthama entered upon him and Al-Mutawakkil said to him, "O Harthama, there is something in my heart about the killing of Ahmad ibn Nasr." Harthama replied, "O leader of the believers, may Allāh cut me into pieces if

---

[82] Translator's note: He is from the students of Imām al-Shafi'ī. He died 240 years after the migration.

[84] Translator's note: Al-Mutawakkil was the 10th Abbasid caliph.

[85] Translator's note: Al-Wāthiq was an Abbasid caliph.

Al-Wāthiq killed him while he was anything other than a disbeliever!" Ahmad ibn Abī Du'ād entered upon him and Al-Mutawakkil said to him, "O Ahmad, there is something in my heart regarding the killing of Ahmad ibn Nasr." He replied to him, saying, "O leader of the believers, may Allāh afflict me with a stroke if Al-Wāthiq killed him while he was anything except a disbeliever!"

Al-Mutawakkil said, "As for Al-Zayyāt, then I burned him to death with fire. As for Harthama, he fled and crossed the Khuzā'a tribe. A man from the neighborhood recognized him and said, 'O Khuzā'a tribe, this is the one who killed your nephew, Ahmad ibn Nasr.' Thus, the tribe seized him and cut him into pieces. As for Ibn Abī Du'ād, then Allāh afflicted him with a stroke four years before his death. His wealth was confiscated, and he fell into deep depression."

In has been collected in the book *The History of Bagdad* by Al-Khatīb al-Bagdadi, that 'Abdul 'Azīz ibn Yahyā al-Kinānī entered upon Ahmad ibn Abī Du'ād while he was suffering from paralysis. He said to him, "Indeed, I did not come here to visit you; rather, I came to praise Allāh for paralyzing your body."

ISMAILI SHIAS

From the stories of the oppressive Batiniyya 'Ubaydis is what was mentioned by Ibn Idhāri. He said, "The first person to establish the da'wah of the 'Ubaidites was 'Abdullāh bin Maymūn al-Qadāh al-Ahwāzi, may Allāh curse him. He claimed prophecy and he had two men as his supporters. One of them was known as Al-Najjār al-Kūfi. They came from Shām and conquered Yemen. Allāh ﷻ afflicted one of the men with an ulcer and he died. As for Al-Najjār al-Kūfī, Allāh inflicted him with a stomach disease, causing his intestines to exit from his anus until he died.

PUNISHMENTS LESS THAN DEATH

From the second category—the punishments in this world that are less than death—there are numerous stories. These incidents occurred at various times, such as in the previous nations, during the pre-Islāmic days of ignorance, after the appearance of the Prophet ﷺ before and after the migration, and some occur up until our present day.

THE TYRANT WHO INTENDED EVIL WITH THE WIFE OF IBRAHIM

From those stories which occurred to the previous nations is the story of Sārah, the wife of Ibrāhīm (the close friend of Allāh ﷺ), and the tyrant who intended to do evil with her. Abū Hurairah ﷺ narrated that the Prophet ﷺ said:

لَمْ يَكْذِبْ إِبْرَاهِيمُ النَّبِيُّ عَلَيْهِ السَّلاَمُ قَطُّ إِلاَّ ثَلاَثَ كَذَبَاتٍ ثِنْتَيْنِ فِي ذَاتِ اللهِ قَوْلُهُ { إِنِّي سَقِيمٌ } وَقَوْلُهُ { بَلْ فَعَلَهُ كَبِيرُهُمْ هَذَا } وَوَاحِدَةً فِي شَأْنِ سَارَةَ فَإِنَّهُ قَدِمَ أَرْضَ جَبَّارٍ وَمَعَهُ سَارَةُ وَكَانَتْ أَحْسَنَ النَّاسِ فَقَالَ لَهَا إِنَّ هَذَا الْجَبَّارَ إِنْ يَعْلَمْ أَنَّكِ امْرَأَتِي يَغْلِبْنِي عَلَيْكِ فَإِنْ سَأَلَكِ فَأَخْبِرِيهِ أَنَّكِ أُخْتِي فَإِنَّكِ أُخْتِي فِي الإِسْلاَمِ فَإِنِّي لاَ أَعْلَمُ فِي الأَرْضِ مُسْلِمًا غَيْرِي وَغَيْرَكِ

Prophet Ibrāhīm ﷺ never told a lie except three times, two times for the sake of Allāh when he said, "I am sick."[86] Also, his words, "Nay, this one, the biggest of them (idols), did it,"[87] and because of Sārah (his wife). He had come in a land inhabited by haughty and cruel men accompanied by his wife Sārah. She was from the most attractive people, so he said to her, "If these people were to know that you are my wife, they would snatch you away from me. So if they ask you, tell them that you are my sister; and in fact you are my sister in Islām, and I do not know of any other Muslim upon the earth besides I and you."

فَلَمَّا دَخَلَ أَرْضَهُ رَآهَا بَعْضُ أَهْلِ الْجَبَّارِ أَتَاهُ فَقَالَ لَهُ لَقَدْ قَدِمَ أَرْضَكَ امْرَأَةٌ لاَ يَنْبَغِي لَهَا أَنْ تَكُونَ إِلاَّ لَكَ . فَأَرْسَلَ إِلَيْهَا فَأُتِيَ بِهَا فَقَامَ إِبْرَاهِيمُ عَلَيْهِ السَّلاَمُ إِلَى الصَّلاَةِ

And when they entered that land, the tyrants came to see her and said to him (the king), "There comes to your land a woman, whom you alone deserve to possess." So, he (the king) sent someone (toward her) and she was brought to him, and Ibrāhīm ﷺ stood in prayer.

فَلَمَّا دَخَلَتْ عَلَيْهِ لَمْ يَتَمَالَكْ أَنْ بَسَطَ يَدَهُ إِلَيْهَا فَقُبِضَتْ يَدُهُ قَبْضَةً شَدِيدَةً فَقَالَ لَهَا ادْعِي اللَّهَ أَنْ يُطْلِقَ يَدِي وَلاَ أَضُرُّكِ . فَفَعَلَتْ فَعَادَ فَقُبِضَتْ أَشَدَّ مِنَ الْقَبْضَةِ الأُولَى فَقَالَ لَهَا مِثْلَ ذَلِكَ فَفَعَلَتْ فَعَادَ فَقُبِضَتْ أَشَدَّ مِنَ الْقَبْضَتَيْنِ الأُولَيَيْنِ فَقَالَ ادْعِي اللَّهَ أَنْ يُطْلِقَ يَدِي فَلَكِ اللَّهَ أَنْ لاَ أَضُرَّكِ . فَفَعَلَتْ وَأُطْلِقَتْ يَدُهُ

When she was entered upon the tyrant king, he came and stretched his hand towards her, and his hand became paralyzed. He said, "Supplicate to Allāh so that He may release my hand and I will do no harm to you." She did so, but then he attempted to touch her again and his

---

[86] Sūrah as-Sāffāt, 37:89.

[87] Sūrah al-Anbiyā, 21:63.

hand became paralyzed more severely than the first occasion. He again requested that she supplicate to Allāh to heal his hand, and she again supplicated, but he attempted to touch her again and his hand was more severely paralyzed than the previous two occasions. He then, again, said, "Supplicate your Lord so that He may set my hand free; by Allāh I shall do no harm to you." She did, and his hand was returned to normal.

وَدَعَا الَّذِي جَاءَ بِهَا فَقَالَ لَهُ إِنَّكَ إِنَّمَا أَتَيْتَنِي بِشَيْطَانٍ وَلَمْ تَأْتِنِي بِإِنْسَانٍ فَأَخْرِجْهَا مِنْ أَرْضِي وَأَعْطِهَا هَاجَرَ . قَالَ فَأَقْبَلَتْ تَمْشِي فَلَمَّا رَآهَا إِبْرَاهِيمُ عَلَيْهِ السَّلاَمُ انْصَرَفَ فَقَالَ لَهَا مَهْيَمْ قَالَتْ خَيْرًا كَفَّ اللَّهُ يَدَ الْفَاجِرِ وَأَخْدَمَ خَادِمًا

Then he called the person who had brought her and said to him, "You have brought to me the devil and you have not brought to me a human being, so expel them from my land." He gave Hajar as a gift to her. She returned (along with Hajar), and when Ibrāhīm ﷺ saw her, he said, "How have you returned?" She said, "With full safety. Allāh restrained the hand of the wicked tyrant, and he gave me a maidservant."[88]

Ibn Kathīr said in *Al-Bidāyah wa Nihāyah*, "I have seen in various narrations that Allāh ﷻ removed the barrier between Ibrāhīm and Sārah. Thus, he was able to see her from the time she departed him until she returned. He saw her while she was with the king, and he saw how Allāh ﷻ protected her from him. This was so Ibrāhīm's heart could be at ease.

---

[88] Sahīh Muslim, 2371.

THE OWNER OF THE TWO GARDENS

From the stories that occurred to the previous nations is the story of the disbelieving man whom Allāh ﷻ gave two gardens of grapes and surrounded both gardens with date-palm trees and put between them green crops. Allāh ﷻ mentioned the conversation between this disbeliever and his believing neighbor in Surah al-Kahf. Allāh ﷻ said:

﴿ وَاضْرِبْ لَهُم مَّثَلًا رَّجُلَيْنِ جَعَلْنَا لِأَحَدِهِمَا جَنَّتَيْنِ مِنْ أَعْنَابٍ وَحَفَفْنَاهُمَا بِنَخْلٍ وَجَعَلْنَا بَيْنَهُمَا زَرْعًا ﴾

And put forward to them the example of two men; unto one of them We had given two gardens of grapes, and We had surrounded both with date-palms; and had put between them green crops.[89]

He mentioned the punishment of the disbeliever:

﴿ وَأُحِيطَ بِثَمَرِهِ فَأَصْبَحَ يُقَلِّبُ كَفَّيْهِ عَلَى مَا أَنْفَقَ فِيهَا وَهِيَ خَاوِيَةٌ عَلَى عُرُوشِهَا وَيَقُولُ يَا لَيْتَنِي لَمْ أُشْرِكْ بِرَبِّي أَحَدًا. وَلَمْ تَكُنْ لَهُ فِئَةٌ يَنْصُرُونَهُ مِنْ دُونِ اللَّهِ وَمَا كَانَ مُنْتَصِرًا ﴾

So his fruits were encircled (with ruin). And he remained clapping his hands with sorrow over what he had spent upon it; while it was all destroyed on its trellises, he could only say, "Would I had ascribed no partners to my Lord!" And he had no group of men to help

[89] Sūrah al-Kahf, 18:32.

him against Allāh, nor could he defend or save himself.[90]

Ibn Kathīr said in *Al-Bidāyah wa Nihāyah*, "Some have said this story is an example, and it does not necessitate that it actually occurred, while the majority say that this story did indeed occur. These two men were companions, one of them was a believer and the other was a disbeliever. Both had wealth. The believer spent his wealth in the obedience of Allāh, while the disbeliever used his wealth for these two gardens. This story shows that whoever gives anything precedence over the obedience of Allāh ﷻ and spending in Allāh's cause, then he will be punished by this thing, and perhaps it will be taken away from him. It also shows how regret will be of no benefit once the decree has befallen."

Owners of the Garden Who Denied the Poor from the Garden

From the stories of the previous nations is the story of the owners of the garden who agreed to prevent the poor access to the garden. Allāh ﷻ mentioned their story in Surah al-Qalam.[91] Ibn Kathīr mentioned in his explanation of these verses, "Some of the Salaf mentioned that these people were from Yemen. Sa'īd ibn Jubayr said, 'They were from a village called Darwān, which is six miles from San'ā (the capital of Yemen). Some scholars have said they were from Abyssinia. Their father left this garden to them, and they were from

[90] Sūrah al-Kahf, 18:42, 43.

[91] Translator's note: This story is mentioned in Sūrah al-Qalam, 68:17-33.

the people of the Book. The father would walk through the garden and extract enough provisions to last his family for the year and give the rest away in charity. When the father died, his sons inherited the garden. They said, 'Our father was foolish when he gave some of our garden to the poor as charity. If we deny the poor access to our garden, then all of it will belong to us.' When they were determined to deny the poor access to the garden, Allāh ﷻ destroyed the garden in its entirety, to include what they had stored away, the profits, and what would have been given in charity. Allāh ﷻ said:

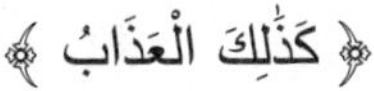

Such is the punishment.[92]

Meaning: such is the punishment for those who oppose the command of Allāh ﷻ and are stingy with the favors Allāh ﷻ has given them, deny the poor their rights and are ungrateful for the blessings of Allāh. Allāh ﷻ said:

﴿ وَلَعَذَابُ الْآخِرَةِ أَكْبَرُ ۚ لَوْ كَانُوا يَعْلَمُونَ ﴾

But truly, the punishment of the Hereafter is greater, if they but knew.[93]

As for the statement of Allāh:

﴿ فَأَصْبَحَتْ كَالصَّرِيمِ ﴾

And it became as though reaped.[94]

---

[92] Sūrah al-Qalam, 68: 33.

[93] Sūrah al-Qalam, 68: 33.

Ibn 'Abbās ﷺ said, "The garden became like a pitch-black night, like black sand."

THE LEPER AND THE BALD MAN

From the stories of what occurred with the previous nations is the story of the leper and the blind man from Banī Isrā'īl. This story has been collected by Bukhārī and Muslim, from the hadīth of Abū Hurairah ﷺ. He heard the Prophet ﷺ saying:

إن ثلاثة في بني إسرائيل أبرص وأقرع وأعمى فأراد الله أن يبتليهم فبعث إليهم ملكاً فأتى الأبرص فقال: أي شيء أحب إليك؟ قال: لون حسن وجلد حسن ويذهب عني الذي قد قذرني الناس, قال: فمسحه فذهب عنه قذره وأعطي لوناً حسناً وجلداً حسناً, قال: فأي المال أحب إليك؟ قال: الإبل, أو قال: البقر, قال: فأعطي ناقة عشراء, فقال: بارك الله لك فيها.

There were three persons in Banī Isrā'īl, one suffering from leprosy, the other bald-headed, and the third one blind. Allāh decided to test them. So, He sent an angel who came to the one who was suffering from leprosy and said, "Which thing do you like most?" He said, "Beautiful color and fine skin, and removal of that which makes me detestable in the eye of people." He wiped him and his illness was removed; and beautiful color and beautiful skin were conferred upon him. He (the angel), again, said, "Which property do you like most?" He said, "The camel (or he said the cow).' Thus, he was given a she-camel in an advanced stage of pregnancy, and while giving this to him he said, "May Allāh bless you in this."

---

[94] Sūrah al-Qalam, 68: 20.

قال فأتى الأقرع فقال: أي شيء أحب إليك؟ قال: شعر حسن ويذهب عني هذا الذي قذرني الناس, قال: فمسحه, فذهب عنه وأعطي شعراً حسناً, قال: فأي المال أحب إليك؟ قال: البقر, فأعطي بقرة حاملاً, فقال: بارك الله لك فيها.

Then he came to the bald person and said, "Which thing do you like most?" He said, "Beautiful hair and that (this baldness) may be removed from me because of which people hate me." He wiped his body, and his illness was removed, and beautiful hair was bestowed upon him, and the angel said, "Which wealth do you like most?" He said, "The cow." He was given a pregnant cow; and while handing it over to him, he (the angel) said, "May Allāh bless you in this."

قال: فأتى الأعمى فقال: أي شيء أحب إليك؟ قال: أن يردّ الله إليّ بصري فأبصر به الناس, قال: فمسحه فردّ الله إليه بصره, قال: فأي المال أحب إليك؟ قال: الغنم, فأعطي شاة والداً, فأنتج هذان وولّد هذا

Then he came to the blind man and said, "Which thing do you like most?" He said, "That Allāh should restore my eyesight so that I should be able to see people." He wiped his body and Allāh restored to him his eyesight, and he (the angel) also said, "Which wealth do you like most?" He said, "The flock of sheep." And he was given a pregnant sheep that gave birth to young ones.

قال: فكان لهذا وادٍ من الإبل ولهذا وادٍ من البقر ولهذا وادٍ من الغنم.

And it so happened that this person had a valley abounded in camels, the other one in cows, and the third one in sheep.

قال: ثم إنه أتى الأبرص في صورته وهيئته فقال: رجل مسكين قد انقطعت بي الحبال في سفري فلا بلاغ لي اليوم إلا بالله ثم بك, أسألك بالذي أعطاك اللون الحسن والجلد الحسن والمال بعيراً أتبلَّغ عليه في سفري فقال: الحقوق كثيرة, فقال له: كأني أعرفك ألم تكن أبرص يقذرك الناس فقيراً فأعطاك الله؟ فقال: إنما ورثت هذا المال كابراً عن كابر, فقال: إن كنت كاذباً فصيّرك الله إلى ما كنت.

He then came to the one who had suffered from leprosy in his previous appearance, and he said, "I am a poor person, and my provision has run short on my journey, and there is none to take me to my destination except with the help of Allāh and then your favor. I beg of you, by the One Who gave you fine color and fine skin and the camel as wealth, that you give me a camel which should carry me on my journey." He said, "I have many responsibilities to discharge." Thereupon he said, "I perceive as if I recognize you. Were you not suffering from leprosy, which people hated, and you were destitute and Allāh conferred upon you wealth?" He said, "I have inherited this property from my forefathers." Thereupon he said, "If you are a liar, may Allāh change you to that very position in which you had been."

قال: وأتى الأقرع في صورته فقال له مثل ما قال لهذا وردّ عليه مثل ما ردّ عليه هذا, فقال: إن كنت كاذباً فصيّرك إلى ما كنت.

He then came to the one who was bald in his (old) form and said to him the same as he said to the one suffering from leprosy. He gave him the same reply as the previous man had given him and he said, "If you are a liar, may Allāh turn you to your previous position in which you had been."

قال: وأتى الأعمى في صورته وهيئته فقال: رجل مسكين وابن سبيل انقطعت بي الحبال في سفري فلا بلاغ لي اليوم إلا بالله ثم بك, أسألك بالذي ردّ عليك بصرك شاة أتبلغ بها في سفري,

Then he came to the blind man in his (old) form, and he said, "I am a destitute person and a wayfarer. My provision has run short, and today there is no way to reach my destination but with the help of Allāh and then with your help. I beg of you, in the (name) of One Who restored your eyesight and gave you the flock of sheep, to give me a sheep by which I should be able to make my provisions for the journey.

فقال: قد كنت أعمى فردّ الله إليّ بصري فخذ ما شئت ودع ما شئت فو الله لا أجهدك اليوم شيئاً أخذته لله. فقال: أمسك مالك فإنما ابتليتم فقد رضي الله عنك وسخط على صاحبيك

He said, "I was blind, and Allāh restored to me my eyesight; you take whatever you like and leave whatever you like. By Allāh, I shall not stand in your way today for the sake of Allāh." Thereupon, he said, "You keep with you what you have in your possession. You three were put to test and Allāh is well-pleased with you, and He is angry with your companions."[95]

Al-Hafidh ibn al-Hajr said in his explanation of Sahīh Bukhārī, "This hadīth is proof that it is permissible to mention situations that have previously occurred so that those who hear of it may benefit from it, and this is not considered backbiting. Perhaps this is the subtle reason for why their names were not mentioned and what occurred to them later in life was not mentioned. But from what is apparent is the supplication of the angel was answered. Therefore, the leper returned to his previous

---

[95] Sahīh Muslim, 2964.

state of leprosy and poverty. The bald man returned to his previous state of baldness and poverty. This was a punishment upon them for opposing Allāh's favor upon them. And there is no doubt that the supplication of the angels is accepted. This is because the angels only act upon the command of Allāh ﷻ.

Those Who Belittled the Sanctity of Mecca and the Ka'bah

Also from the stories of the previous nations is what has been narrated by Al-Azraqī in *The News of Mecca*, from Mujāhid, that a woman was performing tawāf naked around the Ka'bah and she was extremely beautiful. A man saw her and was amazed by her. The man entered tawāf and began to walk next to her so he could touch her. He placed his arm next to her arm and their arms became stuck to one another. They exited the Masjid from the direction of Banū Sahm, fleeing on their faces fearing the punishment that had befallen them. They encountered an elder from the Quraysh as they exited the Masjid. He asked them what happened and they informed him about their situation. He told them to return to the place where they became stuck together and sincerely supplicate to Allāh ﷻ that they would not return to such action. They returned to the place and supplicated to Allāh ﷻ sincerely; and thus, they were separated and each one of them went their separate ways.

It has been narrated in the compilations of 'Abdur Razzāq al-San'ani, with an authentic chain of narration from 'Abdur Rahmān ibn Sābit, "A woman exposed her forearm as she performed tawāf around the Ka'bah during the pre-Islāmic days of ignorance. A man placed his hand on her forearm and his hand stuck to her. An elder advised them to return to the place where he touched her and make an oath to the Lord of the Ka'bah that they would not return to such an action in the future. When they gave this oath, his hand separated from her forearm.

I say these stories contain a lesson and warning for the foolish, those who turn their attention toward women while performing tawāf; thus, they look at the faces of women and their exposed body parts. And perhaps they will flirt with some of the women, or touch some of the women, and some of them perform more heinous acts than this. Some reliable people have mentioned they have seen some evil men following behind women during tawāf; and when they reached a crowded area, they will press up on her from behind. When they saw one particular man doing this, they grabbed him. When they looked at him, they noticed the front of his garment was wet with semen. Thus, they took him to the proper authorities so they could punish him as a deterrent for him, and evil men like him, who do not fear Allāh ﷻ or give any respect to the sanctity of the sacred house. It has also been mentioned to us that some evil men perform tawāf and schedule appointments with women to meet with them and perform indecent acts. There is no doubt that these evil people have exposed themselves to the punishment of Allāh ﷻ in this world, along with the grievous punishment stored for them in the Hereafter if they do not repent from their evil deeds.

The Abducted Boy at the Ka'bah

It has been narrated by Al-Azraqī in *The News of Mecca*, from Ayyūb ibn Mūsā, that during the pre-Islāmic days of ignorance there was a woman who had her young cousin living with her. She would take him out and the people would give her charity because of him. One day she said to him, "O child, I must leave you for a while, but I am afraid someone might oppress you. If an oppressor comes to you when I leave, then indeed, to Allāh ﷻ belongs a house, and there is no house like it. No harm comes near it, and it is covered by a cloth. If an oppressor comes to harm you one day, then seek shelter at that house, for indeed that house has a Lord who hears you." One day, a man came and kidnapped the young boy. During the pre-Islāmic days of ignorance, the people would perform 'umrah. This man performed 'umrah carrying the young boy on his back. When the boy saw the Ka'bah, he recognized its description. He jumped off the man's back, ran towards the Ka'bah and held onto the cloth. The kidnapper reached out his hand to grab the boy, but his hand became paralyzed. He reached out his other hand, and it also became paralyzed. He asked the people what he should do, they told him to sacrifice a camel for each of his hands. He did so, and his hands returned to normal, and he let the boy return home.

The Man and the Antelope

It has been narrated by Al-Fākihi[96] in *The News of Mecca* that 'Abdul 'Azīz ibn Abī Rawād[97] said, "A group of people descended to the Tuwā well in Mecca. Suddenly, an antelope came near to them. A man from amongst them seized the antelope by one of its horns. His companions said to him, 'Woe to you, let it go!' The man laughed at them and re-

[96] Translator's note: He is Muhammad ibn Ishāq al-Fākihi, the historian from Mecca, and scholar of hadīth. He died in the year 279, after the migration.

[97] Translator's note: He was the Imām of Masjid al-Haram in Mecca. He died 159 years after the migration.

fused to let it go. The antelope defecated and urinated, then the man let it go. They all took a midday nap. Some of them awakened to find a snake coiled on the stomach of the man who had harmed the antelope. They said to him, 'Do not move, you have a snake on your stomach!' The snake remained on his stomach until it harmed him equivalent to how he harmed the antelope."

THE MAN WHO LIED ON HIS WIFE

Al-Fākihi narrated that Abū Zur'a said, "I heard Muhammad ibn Abī 'Umar say, 'I heard my father say, "A man had an argument with his father-in-law. The man said to his father-in-law, 'You are the one who brought your daughter to me, and she was not a virgin!' A young boy stood up from the gathering, went to the man's wife and informed her of the statement from her husband. The woman stood, put on her face veil, and then went to the gathering where the argument was taking place. She uncovered her face, looked at her husband, and said, 'O so-and-so, son of so-and-so, do you know who I am?' He responded, 'Yes, you are my wife, so-and-so.' She said, 'Did you say to my father that he brought me to you and I was not a virgin?! O Allāh, if he is lying afflict him with leprosy.' The man was instantly afflicted with leprosy as he sat in his place."

MECCAN BOYCOTT OF THE HASHEMITES

It has been narrated by Ibn Sa'd, from Ibn 'Abbās ﷺ, "The Quraysh wrote a boycott against Banī Hāshim (the tribe of the Prophet ﷺ) that no one should marry women from Banū Hāshim or give them women in marriage, nor should they sell anything to them, buy anything from them, or associate with them. The man who wrote the boycott was Mansūr ibn 'Ikramah al-'Abdari. Ibn Ishāq said, 'The Messenger of Allāh ﷺ supplicated against him and his hand became paralyzed.'"

THE MAN WHO OPPOSED THE COMMAND OF THE PROPHET ﷺ

It has been narrated from the hadīth of Salamah bin Al-Akwa' ﷺ:

أَنَّ رَجُلاً أَكَلَ عِنْدَ رَسُولِ الله بِشِمَالِهِ ، فَقَالَ : كُلْ بِيَمِينِكَ قَالَ: لا أَسْتَطِيعُ. قَالَ : لا اسْتَطَعْتَ! مَا مَنَعَهُ إِلا الكِبْر! فَمَا رَفَعَهَا إِلَى فِيهِ

A man ate with his left hand in the presence of Messenger of Allāh, whereupon he said, "Eat with your right hand." The man said, "I cannot do that." Thereupon he (the Prophet ﷺ) said, "May you not be able to do that." It was arrogance that prevented him from doing it. And he could not raise it (his right hand) up to his mouth afterwards.[98]

[98] Sahīh Muslim, 2021.

In the narration collected by Ahmad [it mentions] that Salamah bin Al-Akwa' ﷺ said, "The Prophet ﷺ said to a man named Busr ibn Rā'ī al-'Īr, whom he saw eating with his left hand, "Eat with your right hand." The man replied, "I cannot do that." Thereupon he (the Prophet ﷺ) said, "May you not be able to do that." Thus, he was not able to put his right hand up to his mouth afterwards.

Imām an-Nawawī said, "This is proof of the permissibility of supplicating against those who oppose the legislated commands without a valid excuse."

I say, "In this supplication of the Prophet ﷺ against the man who opposed his command, and the instant punishment he suffered, is the greatest warning against eating and drinking with the left hand without a valid excuse. So let those who eat and drink with their left hand without an excuse beware, lest they become afflicted with the same punishment that befell Busr ibn Rā'ī al-'Īr, because this punishment is not far off for those who oppose the Messenger of Allāh ﷺ.

THE MAN WHO BELITTLED AN AUTHENTIC HADITH

It has been collected by Ahmad that 'Umar ibn al-Khattab, during his reign as caliph, went out toward the masjid and saw food scattered about. He said, "What is this food?" The people responded, "It was food that was brought to us." 'Umar said, "May Allāh bless it and those who brought it." The people said, "O leader of the believers, it is food which is being hoarded." He replied, "And who is hoarding it?" They said,

"Farrūkh, the freed slave of 'Uthman and so-and-so, the freed slave of 'Umar."

'Umar sent for them and questioned them, saying, "What led you to hoard the food of the Muslims?" They replied, "O leader of the believers, we buy this food with our wealth and then we sell it." 'Umar ﷺ said, I heard the Messenger of Allāh ﷺ say:

مَنِ احْتَكَرَ عَلَى الْمُسْلِمِينَ طَعَامَهُمْ ضَرَبَهُ اللَّهُ بِالْجُذَامِ وَالإِفْلاَسِ

Whoever hoards food from the Muslims (waiting for the price to inflate), then Allāh will afflict him with leprosy and bankruptcy.[99]

Upon hearing this, Farrūkh said, "O leader of the believers, I promise Allāh, and I promise you, that I will never hoard food again."

As for the freed slave of 'Umar, he said, "We buy this food with our money and we sell it." Abū Yahyā said, "Indeed, I saw the freed slave of 'Umar, and he had been afflicted with leprosy."[100]

Also, from the punishments upon those who mocked an authentic hadīth from the Prophet ﷺ is what has been narrated by Al-Dārimi from Ibn 'Ajlān, from Abū Hurairah ﷺ. He said the Messenger of Allāh ﷺ said:

بَيْنَمَا رَجُلٌ يَمْشِي قَدْ أَعْجَبَتْهُ جُمَّتُهُ وَبُرْدَاهُ إِذْ خُسِفَ بِهِ الأَرْضُ فَهُوَ يَتَجَلْجَلُ فِي الأَرْضِ حَتَّى تَقُومَ السَّاعَةُ

[99] Sunan ibn Majah, 2155.

[100] Collected by Al-Bayhaqī in *The Signs of Prophecy*. Ahmad Shakir declared the chain of narration as authentic.

There was a man who used to walk with pride because of his thick hair and fine cloak. He was made to sink in the earth, and he will continue sinking in the earth until the Day of Judgment is established.[101]

Upon hearing this narration, a young man who was wearing a cloak said, "O Abū Hurairah, is this how the man was walking who sunk into the earth?" Then the young man tripped, almost crippling himself. Abū Hurairah ﷺ said, "May he fall on his nose and mouth.

إِنَّا كَفَيْنَاكَ الْمُسْتَهْزِئِينَ

Truly, We will suffice you against the scoffers."[102]

Al-Dārimi placed this in a chapter entitled "Hastening the Punishment upon Those who Hear a Hadīth from the Prophet ﷺ and Do Not Respect It."

From the punishments upon those who mocked authentic hadīth is what has been narrated by Ibn al-Qayyim in his book *The Keys to Happiness*. Ahmad ibn Shu'aīb said, "We were sitting with some scholars of hadīth in Basra. They narrated to us a hadīth of the Prophet ﷺ:

وَإِنَّ الْمَلَائِكَةَ لَتَضَعُ أَجْنِحَتَهَا رِضًا لِطَالِبِ الْعِلْمِ

And indeed, the angels lower their wings, showing pleasure with the student of knowledge.[103]

---

[101] Sahīh Muslim, 2088.
[102] Sūrah al-Hijr, 15:95.
[103] Sunan ibn Majah, 223.

In the gathering there was a man from the Mu'tazila who began to mock the hadīth. He said, "By Allāh, I will wear sandals tomorrow and place nails under them and step on the wings of the angels." The next day, he came with nails in his sandals and began to walk. Both of his legs became paralyzed and were infected with gangrenous sores."

From the punishments of those who mocked authentic narrations is what has been narrated by At-Tabarānī. He said, "I heard Abū Yahyā Zakariya as-Sāji say, 'We were walking in one of the alleys of Basra, heading to sit with some of the scholars of hadīth. We were walking quickly and there was an immoral man amongst us who said mockingly, "Raise your feet from the wings of the angels and do not break their wings." He did not move from his place before his legs were paralyzed and he fell. This has been narrated by Al-Khatīb al-Baghdadi in his book *Traveling in the Pursuit of Knowledge*.

I say, how many are those who mock the authentic hadīth, those who are immoral and tested with hypocrisy, during our time and prior to our time! We have seen many of these statements in their books. Some of these foolish people do not give any value to authentic narrations. They reject authentic narration in the evilest manner, using their shortsighted intellects and evil opinions. There is no doubt that this is waring against Allāh ﷻ and His messenger ﷺ and the followers of the believers. Severe warnings concerning this are found in numerous verses in the Qur'ān. Thus, those who mock authentic hadīth should not feel safe from punishment in this life, in addition to the grievous punishment stored away for them in the Hereafter if they do not repent and accept the statements of the Messenger of Allāh ﷺ with complete acceptance.

THOSE WHO INSULTED THE COMPANIONS

From the punishments of those who insulted the Companions is the story narrated by Ibn al-Qayyim in the book *The Soul.* He said, "It has been narrated by Ibn Abī Dunyā,[104] from Abī Hatīm ar-Rāzi, from Muhammad ibn 'Ālī, that he said, 'We were in Mecca sitting in Masjid al-Haram when a man stood up. Half of his face was black, while the other half was white. He said, 'O people, take a lesson from me. Indeed, I used to insult the two elders. One night, I was sleeping when someone came to me in my dream. He raised his hand, slapped me, and said, "O enemy of Allāh, O sinner, are you not the one who insults Abū Bakr and 'Umar?!" When the morning came, I awakened with my face like this."

It has been narrated by Ibn Sa'd in *Al-Tabiqāt*, from 'Alī ibn Zayd, he said, "Sa'īd ibn al-Musayyib said to me, 'Tell your driver to look at this man's face and his body.' So we looked at a man whose face was black yet his body was white. He said, 'This man used to insult the Companions Talha, Az-Zubayr, and 'Ālī. I advised him and warned him against doing so, but he refused to cease. Thus, I supplicated against him, saying, 'If you are lying, may Allāh darken your face.' Afterwards, an ulcer appears on his face and his face became black.'"

Ibn al-Qayyim narrated that Al-Qayrawani[105] said, "An elder from the virtuous people informed me that the Imām of the Prophet's Masjid said to him, 'I saw something amazing in Madinah. There was a man who used to insult Abū Bakr and 'Umar ﷺ. One day, after the morning pray-

---

[104] Translator's note: He is the noble Imām Abū Bakr 'Abdullāh ibn Muhammad. He died 281 years after the migration.

[105] Translator's note: He is Ibn Abī Zayd al-Qayrawani, born 310 years after the migration.

er, we saw this man and his eyes were protruding from his face on his cheeks. We asked him what had happened to him. He said, 'Last night I had a dream and I saw the Messenger of Allāh ﷺ. 'Ālī was in front of him, along with Abū Bakr and 'Umar. They said, 'O Messenger of Allāh, this is the one who is harming us and insulting us.' The Messenger of Allāh ﷺ said to me, 'Who ordered you to do this, O Abū Qays?' I said to him, "Ālī,' and I pointed toward him. 'Ālī turned toward me, he spread out his fingers, pointed them toward my eyes and said, 'If you are lying, may Allāh protrude out your eyes.' When I awakened from sleep my eyes were like this.' This man would cry, and he informed the people of what happened to him, and he proclaimed his repentance."

From the most heinous punishments is what was narrated by Ibn al-Jawzī in *The Biography of 'Umar ibn al-Khattab*, from Abūl Mahyāh at-Tamīm who said, "The mu'adhin of 'Ālī ibn Abī Tālib said to me, 'I went out with my uncle to Makrān.[106] There was a man with us who would insult Abū Bakr and 'Umar ﷺ. We warned him against doing so, but he did not take heed. We said to him, 'Get away from us!' So he left us. Later, we regretted this and thought we should have allowed him to remain with us until we reached Kūfah. We saw a slave belonging to him and said to his slave, 'Tell your master to return with us.' The slave said, 'Something astonishing happened to my master, his hands were transformed into the hands of a pig!' So, we went to him and asked for him to come and return with us. The man said, 'Something astonishing has happened to me, my forearms have been transformed into the forearms of a pig!' He accompanied us until we reached a village filled with pigs. When he saw the pigs, he let out a scream, jumped down and

[106] Translator's note: This is an area that sits between Pakistan and Iran.

transformed into a pig. He ran into the crowd of pigs, and we no longer saw him. We took his slave and possessions back to Kūfah.'"

This story has been narrated by Al-Lalikā'ī in his book *Explanation of the Sunnah.*

Also from the punishments is the punishment upon those who failed to criticize those who insult Abū Bakr and 'Umar while having the ability to do so. Ibn al-Jawzī mentioned the following story in *The Biography of 'Umar ibn al-Khattab*. "It has been narrated from Abūl Hasan Ahmad ibn 'Abdullāh that he said, 'There was a man next to us who was reading the Qur'ān, known as Abū al-Hasan bin 'Azna, and he differed with our Shaykh Abū al-Hasan bin Abī 'Umar al-Maqri. He spent the night healthy, but when the morning came, he was blind. He was asked about what occurred during the night that caused him to go blind. He said, 'I was in a gathering in Kūfah when a man in the group began to insult Abū Bakr and 'Umar ﷺ. I did not disapprove of the man's statements while I had the ability to do so. When the night came, I saw 'Ālī ibn Abī Tālib ﷺ in a dream. He said to me, 'Why didn't you censure the man who was slandering them?' Then he struck me in the head with a gavel and I went blind.'"

Included in those who were punished in this life is the story of the man from Banī al-'Abas who lied on Sa'd ibn Abī Waqās.

Narrated from Jābir ibn Samurah ﷺ he said:

"The inhabitants of Kūfah complained to 'Umar ﷺ against Sa'd ibn Abī Waqās ﷺ, so 'Umar appointed 'Ammār as Governor of Kūfah in his place. Their complaint was that he did not even conduct the prayers properly. 'Umar sent for Sa'd and said to him, 'O Abū Ishāq, the people claim that you do not offer the prayer properly.' Sa'd replied, 'By Allāh! I observe prayer according to the prayer of the Messenger of Allāh and I make no decrease in it. I prolong standing in the first two rak'ah in Maghrib and Ishā prayers, and shorten in the last ones.' 'Umar said, 'This is what I thought of you, O Abū Ishāq.' Then he sent with him a man or some men to Kūfah to investigate the matter about him from the people of Kūfah. The inquiry was conducted in every masjid, and all the people in these masjids praised him until they entered the masjid of the Banū al-'Abas. A man with the name of Usamah bin Qatadah (and his kunya was Abū Sa'dah) stood up and said, 'Sa'd ibn Abī Waqās did not participate in Jihad, and he did not distribute the spoils equitably and did not judge justly.' On this Sa'd said:

أَمَا وَاللَّهِ لَأَدْعُوَنَّ بِثَلَاثٍ : اللَّهُمَّ إِنْ كَانَ عَبْدُكَ هَذَا كَاذِبًا ، قَامَ رِيَاءً وَسُمْعَةً ، فَأَطِلْ عُمْرَهُ ، وَأَطِلْ فَقْرَهُ ، وَعَرِّضْهُ بِالْفِتَنِ

I shall make three supplications in respect of him: O Allāh! If this slave of Yours is a liar and he stood seeking notoriety and repute, then prolong his life and lengthen his period of poverty and afflict him with trials.

Thereafter, when the man was asked about his condition, he would say, 'I am an old man afflicted with trials and overtaken by the supplication of Sa'd.' 'Abdul-Mālik bin 'Umair said, 'I saw this man with eyebrows hung over his eyes as a result of his old age, and he walked aimlessly, following young girls and winking at them.'"[107]

[107] Sahīh al-Bukhārī, 755.

Worldly Punishment for Backbiting

Ibn al-Qayyim mentioned in his book *The Soul*, in the section on dreams, narrated from Rabī ar-Riqāshi, he said, "Two men came to me, they sat down and started backbiting another man. I forbade them from doing so. Later, one of them came to me and said, 'I had a dream that a black man came to me with a pot of pork meat. I have never seen fattier meat before. He said to me, 'Eat.' I responded, 'Shall I eat pork?!' So, I ate it. When I awakened in the morning, the odor in my mouth had changed, and I continued to taste this odor in my mouth for two months.

The Man Who Harassed the Imam While He Prayed

Among the most heinous punishments is what al-Suyutī mentioned in *The History of the Caliphs*, that in the year 782 a book was received from Aleppo stating the following story, "An imām stood up to pray, and an individual harassed him as he prayed, but the imām continued to pray. When the imām completed the prayer, he turned to the man who harassed him during his prayer and the man's face had transformed into the face of a pig. The man fled to the forest as the people stood in amazement. Those present recorded this event."

The Couples Who Wife-Swapped

Also, from the heinous punishments is what has been narrated to us by the trustworthy person, our neighbor, from Shaykh 'Abdur Rahmān Dawsarī. He narrated to them that a man from a gulf state traveled with his wife to Lebanon. When they arrived in town, they met up with his friend from Lebanon and his wife. They agreed to have sexual intercourse with each other's wives. When the man from Lebanon had intercourse with his friend's wife from the gulf country, his penis became stuck inside of her and he was not able to remove it. They poured hot water on their private parts, but he could not remove himself from her. Then they poured cold water on their private parts, but he still could not remove himself from her. They all became horrified that they could not separate them; thus, they carried them in this evil state to the hospital. They underwent surgery until they removed the man's penis from the woman's vagina.

That is their disgrace in this world.[108]

If they do not repent, the punishment in the Hereafter is greater and longer lasting.

[108] Sūrah al-Mā'idah, 5:33.

THE MAN WHO HARMED 'UTHMAN'S WIFE

Abū Qilābah said, "I was with a group in Shām when I heard a man saying, 'Woe from the Hellfire!' So I went toward him, and there was a man whose arms were cut off from the shoulders, his legs were cut off from the waist, he was blind and lying on his face. I said to him, 'O slave of Allāh, what is wrong with you?' He said, 'I was from those who entered the home of 'Uthman during the Day of the Seize. When I got close to him, his wife came out, so I turned to her and slapped her. 'Uthman looked at me and said, 'May Allāh remove your hands, and your feet, and blind your eyesight and enter you into the Hellfire!' I became terrified of his supplication, so I ran out of his home. When I reached the place I am now, one night Allāh answered his supplication, so I am in the condition you see me in. And the only thing left is his supplication for me to enter the Hellfire.' Abū Qilābah said, 'I considered trampling him with my feet, but I said to him, 'Away with you, go away!'"[109]

THE YOUTH WHO HARMED THE BIRD

Al-Zamakhshari was punished due to the supplication of his mother against him. His story was mentioned by Ibn Khalikān in the book *Deaths of Eminent Men*. It was also narrated by Jamāl al-Dīn, the Copt, in his book *Information of the Narrators*. He said, "Al-Zamakhshari had one leg. He put a stick in place of his missing leg to assist him in walking. When he entered Bagdad, he was asked by the scholar Ad-

[109] Collected by At-Tabari in *The History*, 4/366.

Dāmaghāni[110] the reason his other leg was missing. He responded by saying, 'This is the result of my mother's supplication against me. When I was a youth, I grabbed a sparrow and tied a string to its leg. It tried to fly away and escape from me and I pulled the string; and thus, its leg came off with the string. When my mother saw this, she said, 'May Allāh cut off your leg, as you have cut off the leg of this bird!' When I became older, I traveled to seek knowledge in Bukhara (a city located in Uzbekistan). While traveling, my riding beast fell and crushed my leg, and my leg had to be amputated.'"

THOSE WHO HARMED THE SCHOLARS

From the punishments upon those who harmed the scholars is what occurred to those who altered the chain of narration upon Muhammad ibn 'Ajlān[111]; thus, he supplicated against them and his supplication was answered. His story was mentioned by Imām Dhahabi in his book *Balance in Moderation for Criticizing the Men of Narrations*. Yahyā ibn Sa'īd said, "We arrived in Kūfah while Ibn 'Ajlān was there. Those present seeking knowledge in the city were Mulayh ibn Wakī', Hafs bin Ghiyāth, Ibn Idris, and Yūsūf as-Samti. We said, 'Let us go to Ibn 'Ajlān and switch the chains of narration to test his understanding. All the narrations that Sa'īd narrated from his father, we will say that the father narrated them from Sa'īd. And all the narrations that his father narrated from Sa'īd we will say that Sa'īd narrated them from his father.' Yahyā

[110] Translator's note: He is the noble scholar Abū 'Abdullāh Muhammad ibn 'Ālī ibn Muhammad, born in the city of Damghan, Iran in the year 398 after the migration.

[111] Translator's note: He is from the scholars of hadīth. He died 148 years after the migration.

said, 'I do not agree with doing this.' So they entered upon him and questioned him. When they reached the end of the book, the Shaykh told them to repeat the narrations. When they repeated the narrations, the Shaykh said, 'That which you narrated from the father of Sa'īd was actually from Sa'īd, and that which you narrated from Sa'īd was actually from his father.' He turned to Yūsūf ibn Khalid and said, 'If you intended to shame me, may Allāh strip Islām away from you.' He turned to Hafs and said, 'May Allāh test you within your religion and your worldly life.' He turned to Mulayh and said, 'May Allāh not allow you to benefit from your knowledge.' Yahyā said, 'Mulayh died without benefiting from his knowledge. Hafs was tested in his body by way of a stroke, and he was tested in his religion with the divine decree. Yūsūf did not die until he was accused of heresy.'"

From the punishments upon those who harmed the scholars is what was mentioned by Ibn Bashkuwāl in the biography of Abū Muhammad Makki ibn Abī Tālib al-Muqri.[112] He said, "Abū 'Abdullāh at-Tabari said, 'We were in Córdoba (Spain) and there was a man there who used to harm Shaykh Abū Muhammad Makki al-Muqri. He was standing next to him while the Shaykh was delivering a sermon and winking and counting every slip he made. The Shaykh used to stutter a lot. One day this man came and began staring and winking at the Shaykh. We left and went to another place. The Shaykh continued to read to us and the man followed us. The Shaykh said to us, 'I will supplicate to Allāh and you all say Amīn after my supplication'. The Shaykh said, 'O Allāh, deal with him. O Allāh, deal with him. O Allāh, deal with him.' We all said, 'Amīn.' The man became paralyzed and never entered the masjid after that day."

---

[112] Translator's note: He is the Imām, born in Kairouan in Tunisia, in the year 355, after the migration.

The Punishment of Busr ibn Abi Artat

Busr ibn Abī Artat was punished with insanity after 'Ālī ibn Abī Tālib ﷺ supplicated against him. Al-Mas'ūdi narrated in his book *The Meadows of Gold*, "During the 40th year after the migration, Mu'awiyah sent Busr ibn Abī Artat, along with three thousand soldiers, to Madinah and then to Yemen. Ubaydullah ibn al-'Abbās (the cousin of the Prophet ﷺ) and the cousin of Alī ibn Abī Tālib) was there, and he went to meet with 'Ālī while his two sons, 'Abdur Rahmān and Quthum, followed him, along with their mother Juwayriya bint Qārid. Busr killed 'Abdur Rahmān and Quthum while their mother watched.

When the news reached 'Ālī ibn Abī Tālib ﷺ, he supplicated against Busr, saying, 'O Allāh, remove his religion and his intellect.' Busr became senile and lost his mind. He had been famous for carrying a sword, so when he became senile, they made him a sword of wood to carry, and a sheepskin filled with air was placed in front of him to hit with his wooden sword. Busr died during the reign of Al-Walīd ibn 'Abdul Mālik."

Those Who Said the Qur'an Was Created

From the punishments upon the people of innovation was what occurred to Abū Bakr ibn al-Asam. He was a judge in Egypt during the era of Ibn Abī Dāwūd. He would test the scholars concerning the issue of saying the Qur'ān was created. Those who agreed that the Qur'ān was created would be allowed to go free, those who disagreed would be sent to Ahmad ibn Abī Dāwūd–a proponent of Mu'tazilism in Iraq. When Al-Mutawakkil assumed power, Abū Bakr ibn al-Asam was removed from his position, beaten on his back with a whip, his head and beard was shaved, and he was placed on a donkey and rode around town as the donkey's tail waved in his face.

PUNISHMENT WHICH OCCURRED AFTER DEATH

The second category of punishments are the punishments that occur after death, and these are of two types. The first type are the punishments of many of the people without specifying any specific individual. The second type are the punishments that befell specific individuals who persisted upon their evil until death.

From the first type is what the Messenger of Allāh ﷺ saw during the night journey when he saw sinners being punished for various sins. Also included in this group are those the Prophet ﷺ saw being punished in his dreams. Ibn 'Abbās رضي الله عنه said, "The dreams of the prophets are revelation." Mu'adh ibn Jabal رضي الله عنه said, "The dreams of the Prophet ﷺ are true."

If you understand this, then know that from the punishments the Messenger of Allāh ﷺ saw during the night journey was the punishment of those who eat the flesh of the people and insult their honor.

PUNISHMENTS THE PROPHET SAW DURING THE NIGHT JOURNEY

Anas ibn Mālik ﷺ said, "The Messenger of Allāh ﷺ said:

لَمَّا عُرِجَ بِي مَرَرْتُ بِقَوْمٍ لَهُمْ أَظْفَارٌ مِنْ نُحَاسٍ يَخْمِشُونَ وُجُوهَهُمْ وَصُدُورَهُمْ فَقُلْتُ مَنْ هَؤُلاَءِ يَا جِبْرِيلُ قَالَ هَؤُلاَءِ الَّذِينَ يَأْكُلُونَ لُحُومَ النَّاسِ وَيَقَعُونَ فِي أَعْرَاضِهِمْ

When I was taken up to heaven, I passed by people who had nails of copper and were scratching their faces and their breasts. I said, 'Who are these people, O Jibrīl?' He replied, "They are those who were given to back biting and who defamed people's honor."[113]

From those punishments the Messenger of Allāh ﷺ saw during the night journey is the punishment of the preachers, those who enjoin the people with good while forgetting themselves.

It has been collected by Imām Ahmad, Abū Dāwūd, and Ibn Haban in his collection of authentic narrations from Anas ibn Mālik ﷺ that he said the Messenger of Allāh ﷺ said:

رأيت ليلة أسري بي رجالاً تُقرض شفاههم بمقاريض من نار فقلت: من هؤلاء يا جبريل؟ فقال: الخطباء من أمتك الذين يأمرون الناس بالبر وينسون أنفسهم وهم يتلون الكتاب أفلا يعقلون

During the night journey, I saw men cutting their lips with cleavers made from fire. I said, "Who are they, O Jibrīl?' He said, 'They are the preachers from my nation, those who enjoin the people with piety

[113] Sunan Abi Dawud 4878

while forgetting themselves, while they recite the Book, will they not reflect?"

It has been narrated[114] that the Prophet ﷺ saw Adam ﷺ in the lowest heavens and the souls of his offspring were presented to him. He mentioned the hadīth containing the statement, "Then I proceeded a short distance until I reached a table covered with sliced meat which no one would go near. There was another table with foul smelling meat on it, and there were people eating from this meat. I said, 'O Jibrīl, who are these people?' He said, 'They are those from your nation who abandoned the permissible and went to the impermissible.' I went a little further until I came across people with stomachs like houses, each time they stood up they would fall and say, 'O Allāh, do not establish the Day of Judgment!' He said, 'These people are on the path of the followers of Pharoah.' Then a group came and trampled them. I said: 'O Jibrīl, who are these people?' He said: 'They are from your nation, those who consumed usury; thus, they will not stand except like the one touched by the devil with insanity.' I proceeded a little further and there were people with lips like the mouths of camels. Their mouths opened and hot coals went into their mouths and exited from their bottoms. I heard their crying out to the Allāh ﷻ. I said, 'O Jibrīl, who are these people?' He said they are from your nation. Then he recited the verse:

﴿ إِنَّ الَّذِينَ يَأْكُلُونَ أَمْوَالَ الْيَتَامَىٰ ظُلْمًا إِنَّمَا يَأْكُلُونَ فِي بُطُونِهِمْ نَارًا ۖ وَسَيَصْلَوْنَ سَعِيرًا ﴾

[114] Collected by Al-Bayhaqī in *Signs of Prophecy*.

> **Verily, those who unjustly eat up the property of orphans, they eat up only a fire into their bellies, and they will be burnt in the blazing Fire![115]**

Then I proceeded a little further until I came across a group of women hanging by their breast, screaming out to Allāh ﷻ. I said, 'O Jibrīl, who are these women?' He said, 'These are the fornicators from your nation.' I proceeded a little further until I reached a people who were cutting flesh from their sides and swallowing it. It was said to them, 'Eat, as you used to eat the flesh of your brother!' I said, 'O Jibrīl, who are these people?' He said, 'They are those who used to mock others from your nation.'"

A long hadīth about the night journey of the Prophet ﷺ has been collected by Ibn Jarīr in his *tafsīr* and by Al-Bayhaqī in *Signs of Prophecy*, from the hadīth of Abū Hurairah ؓ. During the night journey, the Prophet ﷺ came across a people whose heads were being smashed with a boulder. Each time their head was smashed, it would return to its normal state, and then it would be smashed again. The Prophet ﷺ said, 'O Jibrīl, who are these people?' He said, 'They are those whose heads were too heavy to perform the obligatory prayers.' Then he came across a people with patches on their backs, roaming about like camels and goats. They were eating thorns and the tree of Zaqūm. The Prophet ﷺ said, 'Who are these people, O Jibrīl?' They are those who did not pay zakat upon their wealth. And Allāh did not oppress them at all, and Allāh does not oppress His slaves.' Then he came across a group of people, and there was a fresh pot of meat in front of them and another pot of meat that was rotten and spoiled. The people began eating from the rotten, spoiled meat and they stayed away from the fresh, good meat.

---

[115] Sūrah an-Nisā, 4:10.

The Prophet ﷺ said, 'O Jibrīl, who are these people?' He said, 'These are men from your nation. They were married to wholesome, permissible women, but they went to filthy women and spent the night with them until morning. And these women were married to wholesome, permissible men, but they went to filthy men and spent the night with them until morning.'"

Included in the punishments the Prophet ﷺ saw is the punishment upon those who consumed usury. Abū Hurairah ؓ said the Messenger of Allāh ﷺ said:

أَتَيْتُ لَيْلَةَ أُسْرِيَ بِي عَلَى قَوْمٍ بُطُونُهُمْ كَالْبُيُوتِ فِيهَا الْحَيَّاتُ تُرَى مِنْ خَارِجِ بُطُونِهِمْ فَقُلْتُ: مَنْ هَؤُلَاءِ يَا جِبْرِيلُ؟ قَالَ: هَؤُلَاءِ أَكَلَةُ الرِّبَا

On the night when I was taken up to heaven, I came upon people whose bellies were like houses and contained snakes which could be seen from outside their bellies. I asked Jibrīl who they were, and he told me that they were people who had practiced usury.[116]

PUNISHMENTS THE PROPHET SAW WHILE DREAMING

It was narrated that Samurah ibn Jundub ؓ said, "The Messenger of Allāh ﷺ often used to ask his Companions, 'Did any one of you see a dream?' So, dreams would be described to him by those who Allāh willed should speak. One morning, the Prophet ﷺ said:

[116] *Mishkat al-Masabih*, 2828.

'Last night, two people came to me (in a dream), and woke me up and said, "Let's go!" I set out with them, and we came across a man who was lying down, with another man standing over him, holding a big rock. He threw the rock at the man's head, smashing it. The rock rolled away, and the one who had thrown it followed it, and picked it up. By the time he came back to the man, his head had been restored to its former state. Then he (the one who had thrown the rock) did the same as he had done before. I said to my two companions, 'SubhanAllāh! Who are these two persons?' They said, "Move on!"

So, we went on, and came to a man who was lying flat on his back, with another man standing over him, holding an iron hook. He put the hook in the man's mouth and tore off that side of his face to the back (of his neck), and he tore his nose and his eye from front to back in a similar manner. Then he turned to the other side of the man's face and did likewise. No sooner had he finished the second side, but the first side was restored to its former state; then he went back and did the same thing again. I said to my two companions, 'SubhanAllāh! Who are these two persons?' They said, "Move on!"

We went on and came to something like an oven.' I think the Prophet ﷺ said in that oven there was much noise and voices. The Prophet ﷺ added, 'We looked into it and saw naked men and women. A flame of fire was reaching them from underneath, and when it reached them, they cried out loudly. I asked them, 'Who are these?' They said to me, "Move on!"

We went on and came to a river. (I think he said, red like blood.) In the river there was a man swimming, and on the bank there was a man who had gathered many stones. While the swimmer was swimming, the man who had gathered the stones approached him. The swimmer opened his mouth and the man on the bank threw a stone into it, then the swimmer carried on swimming. Each time he came back, he opened his mouth again, and the man on the bank threw another stone into his mouth. I said to my two companions, 'Who are these two persons?' They said, "Move on, move on!"

We went on and came to a man who had the most repulsive appearance imaginable. Beside him there was a fire, which he was kindling, and he was running around it. I asked my companions, 'Who is this man?' They said, "Move on, move on!"

We went on until we reached a garden of deep green, dense vegetation, with all kinds of spring colors. In the midst of this garden was a very tall man whose head I could hardly see because of his great height. Around him there were children, a great number such as I have never seen. I said to my companions, 'Who is this man, and who are these children?' They said, "Move on, move on!"

So we went on, until we came to a huge garden, bigger and better than any I have ever seen. My two companions said to me, "Go up." We went up into it, until we reached a city built of gold and silver bricks. We went to the gate and asked for it to be opened. It was opened and we entered the city, where we found men with one side of their bodies more handsome than the most handsome person you have ever seen, and the other side uglier than the ugliest person you have ever seen. My two companions ordered those men to throw themselves into the river. There was a river flowing through the city, and its water was pure white. The men went and threw themselves in the river and came out with the ugliness in their bodies gone, and they were in the best shape. (My two companions) said to me, "This is the Paradise of Eden, and that is your place." I looked up and saw a palace like a white cloud. They said to me, "That is your place." I said to them, "May Allāh bless you both, let me enter it." They said, "For now, you will not enter it, but you shall enter it (one day)."

I said to them, "I have seen many wonders this night. What do all these things mean that I have seen?" They said, "We will tell you. The first man you came across, whose head was being smashed with the rock, is the man who studies the Qur'ān, then he neither recites it nor acts upon it, and he goes to sleep, neglecting the obligatory prayers. The man you came across whose mouth, nose and ears were being torn from front to back, is the man who goes out of his house in the morning and tells a lie that is so serious that it spreads all over the world. The naked men and women whom you saw in a structure that resembled an oven are the adulterers and adulteresses. The man you saw swimming in the river with rocks being thrown into his mouth is the one who consumed ribā (usury). The ugly-looking man whom you saw kindling a fire and walking around it was Mālik, the keeper of Hell. The tall man whom you saw in the garden was Ibrāhīm, and the children around him were the children who died (young) in a state of fitrah (natural state of mankind, i.e., Islām).' Some of the Muslims asked, 'O Messenger of Allāh, what about the children of the pagans?' He said, 'And the children of the pagans too.' 'As for the men who were half handsome and half ugly, they were people who had mixed a good deed with another deed that was bad, but Allāh forgave them.'"[117]

---

[117] Sahīh Muslim, 7047.

Punishments Upon Individuals

As for the punishments upon individuals after death, then this is of three categories. The first category is those mentioned by the Messenger of Allāh ﷺ. The second category is those punishments witnessed by some of the people. And the third category is those punishments seen by some people in their dreams.

From the first category are those the Prophet ﷺ saw as he prayed the eclipse prayer, including the woman who starved the cat, the thief on Hajj, 'Amr ibn Luhay and others.

It has been narrated from Asmā bint Abī Bakr that she said, "The Prophet ﷺ once offered the eclipse prayer. Upon completing the prayer, he said, 'Paradise became near to me that if I had dared, I would have plucked one of its bunches for you; and Hell became so near to me that I said, 'O my Lord, will I be among those people?' Then suddenly, I saw a woman and a cat was lacerating her with it claws. On inquiring, it was said that the woman had imprisoned the cat until it died of starvation; and she neither fed it, nor freed it, so that it could feed itself."[118]

Jābir ibn 'Abdullāh narrated that the Prophet ﷺ prayed the eclipse prayer. After the prayer, he said, "Hell was brought to me; as you saw me moving back on account of fear, lest its heat might affect me. And I saw the owner of the curved staff who dragged his intestines in the fire, and he used to steal the belongings of the pilgrims on Hajj with his curved staff. If the owner of the staff was seen trying to steal, he would say it

---

[118] Sahīh al-Bukhāri, 745.

got accidentally entangled in his curved staff, but if he was not seen, he would take their possessions."[119]

Abū Hurairah ﷺ said, "The Prophet ﷺ said, 'I saw 'Amr ibn Luhay al-Khuzā'i dragging his intestines in the Hellfire, because he was the first man who started the custom of releasing animals for the sake of false gods.'"[120]

From the punishments mentioned by the Messenger of Allāh ﷺ is the punishment of the tale-carriers and those who did not safeguard themselves from urine.

Ibn 'Abbās ﷺ said:

مَرَّ رَسُولُ اللَّهِ . صلى الله عليه وسلم . بِقَبْرَيْنِ جَدِيدَيْنِ فَقَالَ " إِنَّهُمَا لَيُعَذَّبَانِ وَمَا يُعَذَّبَانِ فِي كَبِيرٍ أَمَّا أَحَدُهُمَا فَكَانَ لاَ يَسْتَنْزِهُ مِنْ بَوْلِهِ وَأَمَّا الآخَرُ فَكَانَ يَمْشِي بِالنَّمِيمَةِ

The Messenger of Allāh ﷺ passed by two new graves, and he said, "They are being punished, but they are not being punished for anything major. One of them was heedless about preventing urine from getting on his clothes, and the other used to walk about spreading malicious gossip."[121]

From the punishments mentioned by the Messenger of Allāh ﷺ is the punishment upon the man who stole the mantle during the Battle of Khaybar.

Abū Hurairah ﷺ said, "When we conquered Khaybar, we gained neither gold, nor silver, as spoils of war, but we gained cows, camels,

---

[119] Sahīh Muslim, 904.

[120] Sahīh al-Bukhārī, 3521.

[121] Sunan Ibn Majah, 347.

goods, and gardens. Then we departed with the Messenger of Allāh ﷺ to the valley of Al-Qura, and at that time Allāh's Messenger ﷺ had a slave called Mid'am who had been presented to him by one of Banū Ad-Dibbāb. While the slave was dismounting the saddle of the Messenger of Allāh ﷺ, an arrow—the thrower of which was unknown—came and hit him. The people said, 'Congratulations to him for martyrdom.' The Messenger of Allāh ﷺ said, 'No, by Him in Whose Hand my soul, the sheet of cloth which he had taken illegally on the day of Khaybar from the booty before the distribution of the spoils of war, has become a flame of Fire burning him.' On hearing that, a man brought one or two leather straps of shoes to the Prophet ﷺ and said, 'These are things I took illegally.' On that, the Messenger of Allāh ﷺ said, 'This is a strap (or these are two straps) of Fire.'"[122]

From the punishments mentioned by the Messenger of Allāh ﷺ is the punishment of the man who stole the striped garment. Abū Rafi' ﷺ said, "After the Messenger of Allāh ﷺ had prayed 'Asr, he would go to Banū 'Abdul-Ashhal to speak to them until the time for Maghrib came. While the Prophet ﷺ was hastening to pray Maghrib, we passed by and he said, 'Uff on you, uff on you!' That upset me, so I slowed down because I thought that he meant me. He said, 'What is the matter with you? Keep up!' I said, 'Is there something wrong?' He said, 'Why are you asking that?' I said, 'Because you said, "Uff on you" to me.' He said, 'No, that was so-and-so whom I had sent to collect zakat from the tribe of so-and-so, and he stole a striped garment, and now he is clothed with something similar made of Fire.'"[123]

---

[122] Sahīh al-Bukhārī, 4234.
[123] Sunan an-Nasa'ī, 862.

'Abdullāh ibn 'Amr ﷺ said, "There was a man who looked after the belongings of the Prophet ﷺ, and he was called Kirkira. The man died and the Messenger of Allāh ﷺ said, 'He is in the Fire.' The people then went to look at him and found in his place a cloak he had stolen from the spoils of war."[124]

Anas ﷺ said, "While the Prophet ﷺ was in one of our palm groves where the trees belonged to Abū Talha, he went out to answer the call of nature. Bilāl was walking behind him. The Prophet ﷺ honored him by asking him to walk at his side. The Prophet ﷺ passed by a grave and stood there until Bilāl reached him. He said, 'Woe to you, Bilāl. Did you hear what I heard?' Bilāl replied, 'I did not hear anything.' He said, 'The man in the grave is being punished.' He found that it was a Jew.'"[125]

Anas ﷺ said the Prophet ﷺ said:

لَوْلاَ أَنْ لاَ تَدَافَنُوا لَدَعَوْتُ اللَّهَ أَنْ يُسْمِعَكُمْ مِنْ عَذَابِ الْقَبْرِ

If you were not (to abandon) the burying of the dead (in the grave), I would have certainly supplicated Allāh that He should make you listen the torment of the grave."[126]

Zayd ibn Thābit ﷺ said, "While we were accompanying the Messenger of Allāh ﷺ, who was riding a she-mule in a garden belonging to the Banī an-Najjār, the animal bucked and almost unseated him. There were five or six graves there, so he asked if anyone knew who was buried in them. A man replied that he did. He said they died in the period when

---

[124] Sahīh al-Bukhārī, 3074.
[125] Al-Adab al-Mufrad, 853.
[126] Sahīh Muslim, 2868.

the people were polytheists. The Prophet then said, "These people are being afflicted in their graves, and were it not that you would cease to bury, I would ask Allāh to let you hear the punishment in the grave which I am hearing." Then he turned facing us and said, "Seek refuge with Allāh from the punishment of the Fire." They said, "We seek refuge with Allāh from the punishment of the Fire." He said, "Seek refuge with Allāh from the punishment in the grave." They said, "We seek refuge with Allāh from the punishment in the grave." He said, "Seek refuge with Allāh from trials, both open and secret." They said, "We seek refuge with Allāh from trials, both open and secret." He said, "Seek refuge with Allāh from the trial of ad-Dajjal!" They said, "We seek refuge with Allāh from the trial of Ad-Dajjal."[127]

As for the second category, and it is what has been witnessed by some people of the deceased being punished, it is of two types. The first type is what has been seen and witnessed. The second type is what is heard from the graves. There have been numerous stories narrated for each category. We will mention some of them insha'Allāh.

From the stories of punishments witnessed are the stories of the earth rejecting the bodies of some people after they were buried.

First story: This is the story of the man who apostated after embracing Islām. Anas ibn Mālik ﷺ said, "There was a person amongst us who belonged to the tribe of Banī Najjār. He recited Sūrah al-Baqarah, and Sūrah 'Ālī 'Imrān, and he used to transcribe for the Messenger of Allāh ﷺ. He ran away as a rebel and joined the people of the Book. They gave it much importance and said, "He is the person who used to transcribe for Muhammad, and they were extremely pleased with him. Time passed by and Allāh

[127] *Mishkat al-Masabih*, 129.

caused his death. They dug the grave and buried him therein, but they found to their surprise that the earth had thrown him out over the surface. They again dug the grave for him and buried him, but the earth again threw him out upon the surface. They, again, dug the grave and buried him, but the earth again threw him out upon the surface. At last, they left him unburied."[128]

This story was collected in Sahīh al-Bukhārī with the following wording. Anas ibn Mālik ﷺ said, "There was a Christian who embraced Islām and read Sūrah al-Baqarah and Sūrah 'Ālī 'Imrān, and he used to write the revelation for the Prophet. Later, he returned to Christianity again and he used to say, 'Muhammad knows nothing but what I have written for him.' Then Allāh caused him to die and the people buried him; but in the morning, they saw that the earth had thrown his body out. They said, 'This is the act of Muhammad and his companions. They dug the grave of our companion and took his body out of it because he ran away from them.' They, again, dug the grave deeply for him, but in the morning, they again saw that the earth had thrown his body out. They said, 'This is an act of Muhammad and his companions. They dug the grave of our companion and threw his body outside it, for he ran away from them.' They dug the grave for him as deep as they could, but in the morning, they again saw that the earth had thrown his body out. So, they believed that what had befallen him was not done by human beings and had to leave him thrown on the ground."[129]

Second story: This story has been narrated by from Sumait bin Sumayr, that 'Imrān bin Husain said, "Nafi' bin Azraq and his companions came and said, 'You are doomed, O 'Imrān!' He ('Imrān) said, 'I am not

---

[128] Sahīh Muslim, 2781.

[129] Sahīh al-Bukhārī, 3617.

doomed.' They said, 'Yes you are.' I said, 'Why am I doomed?' They said, 'Allāh says, 'And fight them until there is no more fitnah (disbelief and polytheism), and the religion will be all for Allāh, Alone.'[130] He said, 'We fought them until they were defeated and the religion was all for Allāh, Alone. If you wish, I will tell you a hadīth that I heard from the Messenger of Allāh ﷺ.' They said, 'Did you hear it directly from the Messenger of Allāh ﷺ?'

He said, 'Yes. I was with the Messenger of Allāh ﷺ and he had sent an army of the Muslims to the idolaters. When they met them, they fought them fiercely, and the idolaters gave them their shoulders and ran. A man among my kin attacked an idolator man with a spear, and when he was defeated, the man said, 'I bear witness that none has the right to be worshipped but Allāh. I am a Muslim.' But he stabbed him and killed him. He came to the Messenger of Allāh ﷺ and said, 'O Messenger of Allāh, I am doomed.' He asked him two or three times, 'What is it that you have done?' He told him what he had done and the Messenger of Allāh ﷺ said to him, 'Why didn't you cut open his belly and find out what was in his heart?' He said, 'O Messenger of Allāh, I wish I had cut open his belly and could have known what was in his heart.' He said, 'You did not accept what he said, and you could not have known what was in his heart!'

The Messenger of Allāh ﷺ remained silent concerning him (that man), and a short while later he died. We buried him, but the following morning he was on the surface of the earth. They said, 'Perhaps an enemy of his unearthed him.' So, we buried him again and told our slaves to stand guard. But the following morning he was on the surface of the earth again. Then we said, 'Perhaps the slaves dozed off.' So, we buried

---

[130] Sūrah al-Anfāl, 8:39.

him again and stood guard ourselves, but the following morning he was on the surface of the earth again. So, we threw him into one of these mountain passes. The Prophet ﷺ was told about that and he said, 'The earth accepts those who are worse than him, but Allāh wanted to show you how great is the sanctity of "Nothing has the right to be worshipped except Allāh."'"[131]

Third story: Al-Bayhaqī mentioned this story in the book *Signs of Prophecy*, from the hadīth of 'Usamah ibn Zayd ﷺ. He said the Prophet ﷺ said:

من تَقَوَّل عليَّ ما لم أقل فليتبوَّأ مقعده من النار

Whoever attributes to me something that I have not said, let him take his place in Hell.[132]

He said this because he sent a man on a mission and the man lied upon him. Thus, the Messenger of Allāh ﷺ supplicated against the man. Afterwards, the man was found deceased with his stomach split open, and the earth refused to accept his body.

Fourth story: This story was mentioned by Ibn Idhāri of Marrakesh in his book *Amazing Stories of the History of the Kings of al-Andalus and Maghreb*, in the first volume, on pages 284 to 285. He said, "The cursed one, Al-Jannabi,[133] stole the black stone and sent it to Ubaydullah, the one they believed to be the Mahdi of the Shia. He sent the black stone to him as a gift. A few days later, Ubaydullah died. They buried him in

---

[131] Sunan ibn Majah, 3930.

[132] Sunan ibn Majah, 34.

[133] Translator's note: He is the Iranian warlord Abū Tahir Sulayman al-Jannabi, leader of the Shia sect known as the Qarmatians. He invaded Mecca in the year 930 CE and massacred 20,000 pilgrims.

the ground, but the earth tossed his body out. They buried him three times and each time the earth tossed his body out. His son, Abūl Qasim said, 'This is because he has the black stone, so return it.' They returned the black stone to Mecca, and again buried his body in the same place, and this time the earth accepted his body.

The Continuous Punishment of Abu Jahl

It has been narrated by Ibn Abī Dunyā in *The Book of Graves*, from As-Shabi, "A man said to the Prophet ﷺ, 'I passed by Badr and I saw a man exiting from the ground, and another man struck him in the head with a mallet until he disappeared in the earth. Then he exited again, and the man hit him again until he disappeared. And this occurred several times.' The Messenger of Allāh ﷺ said, 'That was Abū Jahl ibn Hishām, he is being punished until the Day of Judgment.'"

This story has also been collected by Al-Bayhaqī in *Signs of Prophecy* from Ibn Abī Dunyā. He said, "A man came to the Messenger of Allāh ﷺ and said, 'I saw a man sitting at Badr while another man was striking him with a stick made of iron until he disappeared in the earth. The Messenger of Allāh ﷺ said, 'That was Abū Jahl, an angel has been entrusted to strike him each time he exits. Thus, he will continue sinking through the earth until the Day of Judgment.'"

It has been collected by Al-Tabarānī in *Al-Mu'jam al-Awsat* that 'Abdullāh ibn 'Umar ﷺ said, "I was walking close to Badr when I man exited from a pit with a chain around his neck. He called out to me, saying, 'O 'Abdullāh, give me drink!' I do not know if he knew my name or if he was calling me using the custom of the Arabs. Another man exited from the pit with a whip in his hand. He spoke to me, saying, 'Do not give him anything to drink. He is a disbeliever.' Then he beat him with the whip until he returned to his pit. I hurried to the Prophet ﷺ and informed him of what had occurred. He said to me, 'You saw this?' I said, 'Yes.' He said, 'That was the enemy of Allāh, Abū Jahl ibn Hishām, and that is his punishment until the Day of Judgment.'" This story has also been collected by Al-Lalikā'ī in *Explanation of the Sunnah.*

The Continuous Punishment of 'Ubay ibn Khalaf

It has been collected by Al-Bahayqī in *Signs of Prophecy* that Ibn 'Umar ﷺ said, "'Ubay ibn Khalaf died in the middle of Rabigh (a province in Mecca). I was walking in the middle of Rabigh during a windy night, when suddenly a fire began to blaze. A man exited the fire with a chain that was pulling him. He screamed out 'Thirst!' Another man said, 'Do not give him drink. This is the man killed by the Messenger of Allāh ﷺ. This is 'Ubay ibn Khalaf.'"

Translator's addendum: Abū Hurairah ﷺ said, "The Messenger of Allāh ﷺ said, 'The anger of Allāh is most intense against a man who is killed by the Messenger of Allāh for the sake of Allāh (on the battlefield).'" [134]

Al-Nawawī said, "'For the sake of Allāh' excludes one whom he kills as a legal punishment or by way of legal retaliation, because whoever

[134] *Al-Bukhārī*, 4073 and *Muslim*, 1793.

is killed by the Prophet ﷺ on the battlefield was intending to kill the Prophet ﷺ."

It is not known that the Prophet ﷺ killed anyone among the pagans with his own hand, apart from 'Ubay ibn Khalaf. End of translator's addendum.

It has been collected by Hishām ibn 'Ammār[135] in the book *The Resurrection*, from Yahyā ibn Hamza,[136] from Nu'man, from Makhūl,[137] he said, "A man came to 'Umar ibn al-Khattab ؓ. Half of the man's head and half of his beard had turned white. 'Umar asked, 'What happened to you?!' He said, 'I passed by the grave of the tribe of so-and-so one night, and suddenly I saw a man with a whip of fire pursuing another man. Each time he struck him with the whip the man would catch fire from his head to his feet. The man screamed out to me, saying 'O slave of Allāh, give me relief!' The man pursuing him said to me, 'O slave of Allāh, do not give him relief. He is an evil slave of Allāh.' 'Umar ؓ said, 'For this reason, your Prophet hated for any of you to travel alone.'"

The story was also mentioned by Ibn Rajab in his book *Horror of the Graves*.

---

[135] Translator's note: He is the scholar of hadīth. He died 245 years after the migration.

[136] Translator's note: He is the Imām, the scholar. He died 183 years after the migration.

[137] Translator's note: He is from the major Tabi'īn. He died 112 years after the migration.

THE MAN WHO DISRESPECTED HIS MOTHER

It has been collected by Ibn Abī Dunyā in the book *Those Who Lived After Death*, from Mujāhid, that he said, "I went out to take care of some business. While traveling on the road, I was surprised by a donkey. Its neck exited from the ground, and it brayed in my face three times, then entered into the ground. When I reached the people I had intended to meet, they said to me, 'Why has your color changed?' So, I informed them of what I saw. They said, 'This is a youth from the village. That is his mother in that tent. The young man used to drink alcohol. His mother said to him, 'O my dear son, how long will you continue to drink alcohol?' He responded by saying to her, 'You are nothing but a donkey!' Then he would bray in her face three times and laugh. He died that day after 'Asr and we buried him in that ditch. Every day his head comes out of the ditch at the same time we buried him, and he brays three times, like he brayed at this mother. Then he returns to the ditch.'"[138]

FIRE WITHIN GRAVES

It has been collected by Ibn al-Qayyim in the book *The Soul*, he said, "Our companion Abū 'Abdullāh Muhammad ibn ar-Razīz al-Harāni said, 'I left my home after 'Asr, heading toward the orchard. Shortly before sunset, I reached the middle of a graveyard and suddenly I saw a

[138] Translator's note: Al-'Awām ibn Hawshab, from the major scholars of the second generation (died 148 years after the migration), said this narration is sound. It has also been collected by Shaykh al-Albānī in *Sahih Targhīd wa Tarhīb*.

grave with embers and fire exiting from it like a bellow, while the deceased was in the middle of the grave. I wiped my eyes and said to myself, am I sleeping or awake? When I reached the city, I said, By Allāh, I am awake! When I reached the townspeople, I was still in shock. They brought me food, but I was not able to eat. I asked the people about the man in the grave. They informed me he was a tax collector who had died that day.' Ibn al-Qayyim ﷺ said, "Seeing this fire in the grave is similar to seeing the angels and jinn. It happens sometimes to whomever Allāh wants to see them."

From the stories similar to this is what has been narrated to us by our brother for the sake of Allāh, who is the former president of the Islāmic ministry under King Saud ibn 'Abdul 'Azīz 'Ālī Saud. He said, "King Saud sent me to deliver some charity to a remote village in the desert at the top of Najd. We were in the village Ad-Dāth when it was close to sunset, and suddenly we saw a fire from afar. I asked those present about it. They said, 'This fire rises above the grave of a youth from the village of Ad-Dāth.' They informed me that they see this fire every day when sunset is nearby. I asked a trustworthy person about the height of the fire and he told me it was the height of a man or taller. As for the action of the youth—the reason for his punishment and the appearance of the fire above his grave every day—then we do not know the reason. Perhaps he was persistent upon a major sin until his death. And Allāh knows best."

The Woman Who Died Disobeying Her Husband

A story like this was also narrated to me by Shaykh Ismael ibn Muhammad al Ansarī.[139] He said, "We were in the desert of Mali, and there was an African woman who was disobedient to her husband, and she died while being disobedient to him. Every Friday night a great fire would appear from her grave. This fire could be seen from far away, thus the people became distressed due to seeing this fire. One of the elders went to the husband of this woman and request he pardon her regarding his rights over her. The husband refused. They gave him six cows, but the husband still refused to pardon his wife. The husband said, 'I will not pardon her except with the condition that, along with these cows, you give me a *mushaf* written by hand.' He gave them a short time frame to present the handwritten *mushaf* to him. He only stipulated this condition because he thought it would be impossible for them to fulfill. The elder went to some students of knowledge and gave them papers to write the *mushaf* on. They wrote out the *mushaf* before the time stipulated by the husband. The elder gave the *mushaf* and the six cows to the husband, and he forgave his wife and considered this to be his wife fulfilling his rights. But he only did so because he was embarrassed to renege on his agreement, due to the respect he had for the elder." Shaykh Ismael said, "We did not see the fire after that." Shaykh Ismael informed me that he had seen the fire himself.

---

[139] Translator's note: Shaykh Ismael al-Ansarī is from the scholars of hadīth. He was born in the Sahara Desert in the year 1921 CE. Shaykh Sālih Luhaydan said about him, "He is the former president of the Supreme Judicial Council, and he is of sound aqīdah. Shaykh Ismael died in 1996 CE.

THE WOMAN WHO DIED PERSISTENT UPON THREE SINS

A similar story was narrated to me by a reliable man named Sālih ibn Muhammad al-Muqaitaib. He said that he went out to a large cemetery in the city of Riyadh. It is known as the Oud Cemetery. This occurred on a Friday, on the 17th day of the month of Muharram, in the year 1392 AH (1973 CE). He went to the cemetery shortly after Jum'āh prayer to visit some deceased family and friends. He said, "While I was in the graveyard, a funeral procession arrived with a deceased woman. I assisted them in burying her. After we had placed dirt in the grave and there were only about four handfuls of dirt remaining to cover the grave, the father of the deceased woman—who was an elderly man—said, 'I dropped the keys to my money chest in the grave, and there is a large sum of money buried with her.' Then he began digging up the dirt from the grave. Those who were with him had no good in them, so they abandoned him and did not help him. When I saw that action from them, I started to help him remove the dirt from the grave. We removed the dirt and searched, but did not find any keys nor any money. When there was nothing remaining except the niche in the grave, I exited the grave and went to visit some other graves. The smell from the woman's father had bothered me, due to his sweating while digging the grave and because he smoked a filthy tobacco called al-Jarak.[140] So, the smell from his mouth was harming me; therefore, I exited from the grave. When I got a short distance away from him, I heard a sound which sounded like a stone thrown on soft clay. This sound was followed by a loud scream from the man. So, I returned to him and found

[140] Translator's note: Al-Jarak is tobacco to which a group of rotting fruits are added.

that he had fallen into the grave, lying on his back, with his head facing south and his feet facing north. He was rubbing his neck and his throat with his hands while screaming, 'Put out the fire!' I took a bucket of water and poured it on him, and it died down. Then we took him out of the grave. He was not moving at all. I did not know if he was alive or dead. His companions carried him off to his home in the coffin in which his deceased daughter had been brought in.

No one remained in the graveyard other than me and two people who came with the funeral procession. One of them was an elderly man and the other was a young boy. We returned to the grave to find that the father of the woman had moved the brick under the woman's head. So, I entered the grave to put the brick back under her head. When I entered the grave, I saw that the shroud covering the woman's head had become black like coal. This was the only part of the shroud that I could see because the rest of the shroud was hidden from me by the plank of wood. In the niche of the grave facing the woman's neck, there were two blue lines tinged with a little bit of yellow, and their width and the separation between them was about three fingers. I became terrified, such that I urinated on my garment without realizing it, until I felt urine running down my thigh and shin. We covered the grave with dirt again. I asked the elderly man concerning the deceased woman and her family, but he refused to tell me anything. I took the young boy by the hand and walked with him to the side of the cemetery and asked him. He informed me that the deceased woman was his paternal aunt. He said she was deserving of everything that happened to her. I asked what was her condition? He said, 'She would sit in front of the television and not pray until her program was over. Her mother would forbid her from delaying the prayer outside of its time, but she would not listen. One day her mother came, and the daughter had delayed the prayer past its time, so the mother kicked the television and it fell and busted open. So she got up in her mother's face, angry, and quarreling with her and reprimanding her for what she had done. She wanted to repair the television, so her father took her to repair it.' He then asked the boy if the woman had any children, and the boy said no. She had been married and was now divorced for over a year, and she did not remarry." This is the end of what Sālih narrated to me.

This woman combined three impermissible actions. Firstly, she was lackadaisical with regard to the prayer. She delayed the prayer until after its fixed time and she preferred her entertainment. Secondly, she disobeyed the command of her mother, when her mother told her to pray during the fixed prayer times. Thirdly, she made these amusements permissible and preferred them over the obedience of Allāh ﷻ. Her father was afflicted with a portion of the punishment because he supported her evil action and took her to repair her amusement device that had distracted her from the remembrance of Allāh ﷻ and the prayer. Also, the father smoked the filthy tobacco called al-Jarak, and it is an intoxicant. Everything that intoxicates is considered alcohol. The Messenger of Allāh ﷺ said:

مُدْمِنُ الْخَمْرِ إِنْ مَاتَ لقيَ اللهَ كعابِدِ وثن

The person addicted to alcohol, if he dies in that state, he will meet Allāh like an idol worshipper.[141]

Thus, take a lesson, those who are lackadaisical with regard to the prayer by delaying the prayer until after the time has ended, this sin allowed this woman to be punished in her grave. And take a lesson, those who permit listening to musical instruments, that which distracts you from

---

[141] *Mishkat al-Masabih*, 3657.

the remembrance of Allāh and the prayer. This punishment is not far off from the disobedient.

FIRE FROM THE CASKET OF THE SHIA

It was narrated to me from Sālih ibn Muhammad al-Muqaitaib. He said, "When this story of this woman punished in her grave spread, a man came to me from Pakistan. This man works in one of the business institutions in Riyadh. The man asked me about the story of the woman, and I informed him of what occurred. He said, 'Something similar happened in Pakistan.' A major merchant from the Shia was near death, and he entrusted his family to take him to Najaf (a city in central Iraq) to bury him there. When he died, they placed his body in a casket and put his casket under the shade of a tree in the garden of his home. They placed air conditioners around his casket, so his corpse would remain the same until the plane arrived to transport his body to Najaf. The plane was late and did not arrive for a number of days. When they wanted to transport him, they removed the covering of the casket so they could see if the deceased's body had changed or not. When they opened the casket, a flame shot out, burning the top of the casket and the branches of the tree. The body of the deceased was in the same state it was when they placed him in the casket."

I say there is no doubt that the deceased person who has fire exiting from his grave is being punished, even if the living does not see the effects of it. This is because this is the fire of the Hereafter, and the people of this world may not perceive its effects upon the dead, although it is several times hotter than the fire of this world.

Ibn al-Qayyim said in the book *The Soul*, "Indeed, the fire within the grave, and the meadow within the grave, are not similar to the fire of this world nor the pastures of this world. Therefore, the punishment and bliss in the grave is not perceived by those who perceive the fire and pastures of this world. The fire within the grave is more severe in heat than the fire of this world. Allāh ﷻ shields the dirt and stones over the grave; so although the fire in the grave is hotter than the fire on this world, if the people touch the dirt they will not feel the heat. Rather, what is more amazing than this is: two men are buried next to each other; this grave is a pit of fire, but its heat does not reach the grave next to him. The grave next to him is a garden from the gardens of Paradise, but its fragrance and bliss does not reach the grave next to it. The ability of the Lord ﷻ is more expansive and more amazing than even that. Indeed, Allāh ﷻ has shown us from the signs of His power in this world that which is much more amazing than that. However, the souls are inclined toward rejecting and denying that which their knowledge does not comprehend, except for those whom Allāh grants success and those whom He protects. Two sheets of fire are spread out for the disbeliever. They ignite his grave like a furnace is ignited. If Allāh ﷻ wills, He will reveal this to some of His slaves and conceal it from others. If Allāh revealed this to all of His slaves, the test of believing in the unseen would be removed and the people would not bury one another. The Messenger of Allāh ﷺ said:

لَوْلاَ أَنْ لاَ تَدَافَنُوا لَدَعَوْتُ اللَّه أَنْ يُسْمِعَكُمْ عَذَابَ الْقَبْرِ

Were it not that you would not bury one another, I would have prayed to Allāh to make you hear the torment of the grave.'[142]

---

[142] Sunan an-Nasa'ī, 2058.

Because this wisdom does not apply to the animals, they are able to hear and perceive this. Likewise, the Messenger of Allāh ﷺ was able to hear this when he passed by the graves." End of Ibn al-Qayyim's speech.

THE WOMAN WHO DELAYED THE PRAYER AND SPIED ON HER NEIGHBORS

Ibn Abī Dunyā narrated that 'Amr ibn Dinar[143] said, "A man from Madinah had a sister that passed away. They prepared her body and carried her to the grave. After they buried her, they returned to their family. The man remembered that he forgot a bag inside of the grave. He took one of his companions with him to retrieve the bag. They dug up the grave and found the bag. The man said, 'Let us check the condition of your sister.' They removed the plank covering the niche and found her grave ignited with fire. They covered the grave back with dirt and went to his mother to ask her about the condition of his sister. The mother said that she would delay the prayer until its time elapsed and she did not believe she would perform *wudhu* before praying. She would also go to the door of her neighbor when everyone was asleep and place her ear at their door to eavesdrop on their conversation."

I say in this story is a lesson and warning for those who delay the prayer until its time goes out, and those who are not concerned with properly performing *wudhu* for the prayer. This is also a warning and lesson for those who spy on the people and listen to their secrets and speech

[143] Translator's note: 'Amr ibn Dinar was from the scholars of hadīth from the second generation of Muslims. He was from the students of the noble Companion Ibn 'Abbās.

which they do not want others to hear. And how lowly are these types of people!

THE DECEASED WITH A RING OF FIRE AROUND HIS NECK

It has been narrated by Safārini[144] in the book *Al-Buhūr Az-Zākhiratu* that he said, "Ibn Rajab and others narrated that a group from the Tābi'īn went to visit Abī Sinān,[145] and when they reached him, they sat with him. He said, 'Go with us to visit our neighbor whose brother died, so we can give him condolences.' Muhammad ibn Yūsūf al-Firyābi[146] said, 'We went with him to visit the man and found him crying profusely, and he was extremely alarmed at the death of his brother. We gave him condolences and tried to console him, but he could not be consoled. We said to him, 'Are not you aware that death is inevitable?' He responded, 'Of course, but I cry due to the punishment my brother endures each morning and evening.' We said to him, 'Has Allāh reveal to you the unseen?' He said, 'No, but when I buried him and placed dirt over his grave, the people left, but I sat by his graveside. Then I heard a voice from his grave saying, 'Ah! Leave me alone to suffer the torment. I used to pray, I used to fast!' Therefore, I cry due to hearing his words. And I said, by Allāh, I know my brother's voice. I said, perhaps I am imagining this. He became quiet, and then I heard a second voice and

---

[144] Translator's note: He is Muhammad bin Ahmad al-Saffārini. He died 1774 CE.

[145] Translator's note: He is Hassān ibn Abī Sinān.

[146] Translator's note: He is a scholar of hadīth and companion of Sufyān at-Thawrī. He died 212 years after the migration.

third voice screaming that I did not recognize. I began to dig up his body. When I got close to the niche, I saw a ring of fire around the middle of his neck. I put my hand on it, hoping to break it; but I burnt my finger, so I quickly pulled my hand away. I, again, covered his grave with dirt and left. So how can I not cry and be sad due to the condition I saw him in?'

We asked him, 'What did your brother used to do while he was alive?' He said, 'He did not pay zakat upon his wealth.' We said, 'This coincides with the statement of Allāh ﷻ:

﴿ وَلَا يَحْسَبَنَّ الَّذِينَ يَبْخَلُونَ بِمَا آتَاهُمُ اللَّهُ مِن فَضْلِهِ هُوَ خَيْرًا لَّهُم ۖ بَلْ هُوَ شَرٌّ لَّهُمْ ۖ سَيُطَوَّقُونَ مَا بَخِلُوا بِهِ يَوْمَ الْقِيَامَةِ ﴾

> **And let not those who covetously withhold of that which Allāh has bestowed on them of His bounty think that it is good for them (and so they do not pay the obligatory zakat). Nay, it will be worse for them; the things which they covetously withheld shall be tied to their necks like a collar on the Day of Resurrection.'**[147]

We said to him, 'The punishment for your brother has been hastened in his grave.' Then we left him.'

Muhammad ibn Yūsūf al-Firyābi said, 'I said to al-Awzā'i[149], 'The Jews and Christians die, and we do not see or hear this from their deceased?' He said, 'As for them, there is no doubt that they are in the Hellfire.

[147] Sūrah 'Ālī 'Imrān, 3:180.

[149] Translator's note: He is the well-known scholar and Imām Abū 'Amr 'Abdur Rahmān ibn 'Amr al-Awzā'i. He died 157 years after the migration.

Allāh only shows you the punishment of the believers to serve as a lesson and admonition for you.'"

The Man Who Sinned While in Seclusion

Ibn Hajr al-Haytami mentioned in his book *A Rebuke Against Committing Major Sins* that 'Abdullāh ibn Zayd said, "The moon allured me, so I went for a walk and passed by a graveyard. Suddenly, there was a man exiting from his grave, dragging a chain. Another man was behind him holding on to the chain until he dragged him back into his grave. I heard him beating him while the man was saying, 'Did I not used to pray? Did I not used to purify myself from major impurities? Did I not used to fast?' The other man responded, 'Of course, but when you were alone you indulged in sin, and you were not cognizant that Allāh ﷻ was observing you.'"

The Man Who Performed Hajj with Pilfered Wealth

It has been narrated by Al-Lalikā'ī in his book *Explanation of the Sunnah*, from Sadaqah ibn Khalid, from Damascus, from some of his scholars that he said, "We performed Hajj and a man who accompanied us died on the road near the water. We went to the people who lived near the water to request something to dig a grave for him. They gave us an axe and a shovel. After we had buried him, we realized we had left the axe inside the grave. When we dug up his grave we found his neck, his hands and his legs bound to the axe handle. We covered him back up and gave the people the money to cover the price of the axe. We left and went to his wife and asked her concerning him. She said he had accompanied a wealthy man, killed him, stole his money, and used it to perform Hajj."

THE MAN WHO INSULTED THE COMPANIONS

Ibn Abī Dunyā narrated from Abī Ishāq that he said, "I was summoned to a deceased man to wash his body. When I removed the covering from his face, there was a snake wrapped around his neck. I left without washing him. No one saw this besides me. It was mentioned that he used to insult the Companions."

'UBAYDULLAH IBN ZIYAD, THE KILLER OF HUSAYN IBN 'ALI

Umārah ibn Umayr said, "When the heads of 'Ubaydullah ibn Ziyad and his companions were brought, they were stacked in the masjid at Ar-Rahbah. So, I came to them and they were saying, 'It has come, it has come.' And behold, there was a snake going between the heads, until it entered the nostrils of 'Ubaydullah bin Ziyad. And it remained there momentarily, then left and went until it had disappeared. Then they said, 'It has come, it has come.' So it did that two or three times."[150]

THE DECEASED WITH IRON NAILS IN HIS BODY

Ibn Abī Dunyā said 'Abdul Mu'min ibn 'Abdullāh al-Qaysi narrated to us, "It was said to a graverobber who had repented, 'What is the most amazing thing you have seen?' He said, 'I dug up a man and saw nails covering his entire body, a huge nail in his head and nails in his feet.' Another graverobber was asked about the most amazing thing he saw. He said, 'I saw the skull of a human riddled with iron pellets.'"

DECEASED TURNED AWAY FROM THE QIBLA IN THEIR GRAVES

Ibn Abī Dunyā said, "A man narrated to me that his daughter died and he buried her. When he went back into the grave to repair a brick, he noticed that her body had been turned away from facing the Qibla prayer direction. This made him extremely sad. He saw her in a dream, and she said to him, 'O my dear father, I became sad when I saw that most of the people in the graves around me have been turned away from the

[150] Collected in Tirmidhī, declared authentic by Al-Albānī.

Qibla.' He said, 'I believe she meant those who died while being persistent upon major sins.'"

THOSE WHO DIED UPON OTHER THAN THE SUNNAH

Ibn Abī Dunyā said a man asked Abū Ishāq al-Fazāri[151] if a graverobber can repent. The man said to him, "I used to be a graverobber and I used to find people in their graves with their faces facing away from the Qibla." Al-Fazāri did not have anything to tell the man; therefore, he wrote to Al-Awzā'i to ask him. Al-Awzā'i wrote to him, "His repentance is accepted if his intention is correct, and Allāh knows his heart is sincere. As for his saying that he found these deceased people with their faces turned away from the Qibla, these are people who died upon other than the Sunnah."

I say many people are turned away from the Qibla in the graves, and they are those who died smoking filthy cigarettes without repenting.

THOSE WHO DIED ADDICTED TO SMOKING

One of our trustworthy brothers said to me, "A traveler came to our town and became sick. He remained with us for a number of days, then

[151] Translator's note: He is Abū Ishāq Ibrāhīm ibn Muhammad ibn al-Hārith. He died 183 years after the migration.

death came near to him. I turned him toward the Qibla, then he turned away from it. Each time I turned him toward the Qibla, he would immediately turn away from it. This happened numerous times. The final time it was extremely difficult to turn his body toward the Qibla. I exerted all my efforts to turn his head and body toward the Qibla, but I was unable to do so. Therefore, I left him facing the opposite direction. His soul left his body while he was facing opposite to the Qibla. I was surprised that I was unable to turn him. When I looked through his belongings, I found a pack of tobacco and the device he used to smoke it with."

Some of my scholars narrated to me that Shaykh Muhammad ibn 'Abdul Latīf ﷺ [152] said they were traveling from Mecca to Madinah, and there was a man from Qatar with them. The man used to pray a lot and do many acts of good, but he used to smoke. He died on the road, and they turned him toward the Qibla. But each time they turned him to face the Qibla, he would turn away from it.

Likewise, some of our scholars narrated to us that Shaykh 'Uthman ibn Bishr,[153]who was a judge in Qasim, informed them that a man died while in their presence. This man used to pray a lot and the only criticism of him was that he smoked. Shaykh 'Uthman said, "I descended into the grave, placed him in the niche, and turned his body toward the Qibla. When I reached up to grab the plank of wood to place over the niche, his body had turned away from the Qibla such that his back was

---

[152] Translator's note: He is the noble scholar Shaykh Muhammad ibn 'Abdul Latīf 'Ālī Shaykh. He died in the year 1947 CE. His students include Shaykh Muhammad Ibrāhīm, the former Grand Mufti of Saudi Arabia, and Shaykh 'Abdul 'Azīz ibn Baz, the former grand mufti of Saudi Arabia.

[153] Translator's note: Shaykh 'Uthman ibn 'Abdullāh ibn 'Uthman al-Bishr died 1873 CE.

facing the Qibla. Each time I faced him toward the Qibla, his body would turn toward the other direction. After the third time, I left his body facing away from the Qibla."

Sālih ibn Muhammad al- Muqaitaib narrated a story to me about a man who used to smoke. He said, "I was sitting in my shop one Friday morning when so-and-so passed by me. I closed my shop, took him to my home, and prepared some tea and coffee for him. When he wanted to drink the tea, he pulled out a pack of cigarettes from his pocket to smoke. I prevented him from smoking in my home and said to him, 'If you go outside of my home, then what you do is up to you.' After he drank the coffee and tea, he went outside of my home. Shortly after he left my home, someone knocked on my door and informed me that the man who had left my home died suddenly. I took him for washing and shrouding. After Jum'āh prayer, we performed the funeral prayer over him and took his body to the cemetery. We placed his body within the niche in the grave facing the Qibla, but his body turned away from the Qibla. Those present, including me, saw his body turn away from the Qibla."

MOANS FROM THE GRAVE

Shaykh Ismael ibn Muhammad al-Ansārī said to me, "We were in the desert of Mali in Africa. A youth who was disobedient to his parents died. We heard moaning sounds coming from his grave, so we dug him up thinking we had buried him alive. When we dug him up, we found him deceased and shrouded just as we had buried him. But we continued to hear moaning coming from his grave after we put dirt over his grave again."

Punishments Seen in Dreams and Unconsciousness

As for the third section, it is what a person sees in a dream or what they see when they faint, from the torture of the people of innovation and those who persist in the darkness of sins. There are numerous stories in this category. It has been collected by Ibn Abī Dunyā that Ahmad ibn Jamīl said 'Abdullāh ibn al-Mubārik said 'Abdur Rahmān ibn 'Abdullāh ibn Dinar narrated that Zayd ibn Aslam said, "Al-Miswar ﷺ fainted. When he awakened, he said, 'I testify that nothing has the right to be worshipped except Allāh, and Muhammad, the Messenger of Allāh, is more beloved to me than the entire world and everything in it. 'Abdur Rahmān ibn Awf is in the highest level of Paradise with those Allāh is pleased with from the prophets, the truthful, the martyrs, and the righteous; and what a wonderful group this is. And 'Abdul Mālik and Al-Hajjaj are dragging their intestines in the Hellfire.'"

Ibn Hajr mentioned this story in the biography of Al-Hajjaj ibn Yūsūf, then he said, "This chain of narration is authentic. And at the time this statement was made, Al-Hajjaj had not been known and 'Abdul Mālik had not been placed as caliph yet. This is because Al-Miswar died the day the death announcement was given for Yazid ibn Mu'awiyah from Shām. And that was during Rabī' al-Awwal, during the year 64, after the migration.

Al-Hajjaj ibn Yusuf's Punishment

It has been collected by Abū Nu'aym[154] in his book *Al-Hilyat*, in the biography of 'Umar ibn 'Abdul 'Azīz ﷺ [155]. He said, "'Umar fainted. While he was unconscious, he saw a vision that the Day of Judgment had begun, and he was standing in front of Allāh ﷻ. Allāh bestowed mercy upon him and commanded him to enter Paradise. He said, 'As I was walking between the two angels entrusted to me, I passed by a corpse which had been flung on the desert ground. I said, 'Whose corpse is this?' They said, 'Get closer, ask him, and he will tell you.' I got close to him, kicked him with my foot, and said, 'Who are you?' He responded to me by saying, 'Who are you?' I said, 'I am 'Umar ibn 'Abdul 'Azīz.' He asked, 'What has Allāh done with you and your companions?' I said, 'As for four of us, Allāh commanded us to enter Paradise. I do not know what happened to those after that.' He said, 'I am as you see.' I said, 'Who are you?' He said, 'I am Al-Hajjaj ibn Yūsuf.' I said, 'What has Allāh done with you?' He said, 'My Lord has given me a severe punishment. He is severe in might, and He takes revenge upon those who disobey Him. He killed me in every way that I killed someone previously. Now I will stand before my Lord and wait for what every person who dies upon *tawhīd* waits for, either the Fire or Paradise.'"

This story was also mentioned by Ibn al-Jawzī in the biography of 'Umar ibn 'Abdul 'Azīz.

---

[154] Translator's note: He is Abū Nu'aym Ahmad ibn 'Abdullāh al-Isfahāni, a Muslim historian who died the year 430, after the migration.

[155] Translator's note: He is the noble leader, the 8th caliph, 'Umar ibn 'Abdul 'Azīz. He died 101 years after the migration.

Bishr al-Marisi

It has been collected by Al-Khatīb in his collection of *The History of Bagdad* that 'Abdullāh ibn al-Mubārik said, "I saw Zubaidah[156] in a dream. I asked her, 'What has Allāh done with you?' She said, 'He forgave me when the first axe struck the road to Mecca.'[157] I said to her, 'What is that yellow streak I see on your face?' She said, 'Buried behind me is a man named Bishr al-Marisi, the Hellfire let on a growl upon him, causing my skin to shiver. This yellow streak was caused by that growl.'"

Ibn Abi Dawud the Mu'tazilite

It has been collected by Al-Khatīb, from Sufyān ibn Wakī', he said, "I had a dream in which I saw the Hellfire growling and flames exiting from it. I said, 'What is this!' It was said, 'This is prepared for Ibn Abī Dāwūd.'"

[156] Translator's note: She is Zubaidah bint Jafar, the wife of Caliph Harūn Rashid.

[157] Zubaidah improved the 900-mile stretch of road between Kūfa and Mecca. With her wealth, she cleared and paved the road and added water reservoirs.

The Man Who Denied the Divine Decree

It has been collected by Al-Ajurri[158] in the book *Sharī'a* that Abū Ghiyāth said, "While I was washing the body of a man who denied the Divine Decree, those assisting me left and I was alone. I said, 'Woe to those who deny the decree of Allāh!' His body fell off the washing table. We buried him in the Muslim cemetery at Bab al-Sharqi. I saw myself in a dream that night, leaving the masjid. There was a funeral procession in the marketplace, and two Abyssinian men were being carried in front of the people. I said, 'Who is this?' They replied, 'This is so-and-so.' I said, 'Allāh is free from imperfection! Did we not just bury him at Bab al-Sharqi?' They said, 'You buried him in the wrong place.' I said to myself, 'By Allāh, I will follow them until I see what they do with him.' They took him inside the cemetery from the gate of the Jews, placed his body in a Christian sarcophagus,[159] and buried him there. His legs protruded and they had become darker than the night."

Those Who Believed in the Unity of Existence

From the story of those who believed in the unity of existence is what was mentioned by Shaykh al-Islām Abūl 'Abbās ibn Tamiyyah ﷺ. He said, Shaykh Ibrāhīm al-Ja'bari said, "I saw in a dream ibn Arabi[160] and

---

[158] Translator's note: He is the Imām Abū Bakr Muhammad ibn al-Husayn. He died 320 years after the migration.

[159] Translator's note: A Christian casket carved from stone and laid above ground.

[160] Translator's note: A Sufi mystic and poet who died 638 years after the migration.

Ibn al-Fārid[161] as two elderly, blind men stumbling about, asking 'Where is the path, where is the path?'"[162]

THE OBLIGATION OF BELIEVING IN THE BLISS AND PUNISHMENT OF THE GRAVE

If you have understood from the previous stories of those punished in the grave that Allāh ﷻ may reveal to some of the living some punishments of the deceased, then also understand that it is obligatory to believe in the bliss and punishment of the grave. The bliss in the grave is for the righteous. The punishment of the grave is from the disbelievers, hypocrites, and those who died upon major sins without repentance. The Messenger of Allāh ﷺ said:

إِنَّمَا الْقَبْرُ رَوْضَةٌ مِنْ رِيَاضِ الْجَنَّةِ أَوْ حُفْرَةٌ مِنْ حُفَرِ النَّارِ

The grave is either a garden from the gardens of Paradise or a pit from the pits of the Hellfire.[163]

'Uthman ibn Affan ﷺ said the Messenger of Allāh ﷺ said:

إِنَّ الْقَبْرَ أَوَّلُ مَنْزِلٍ مِنْ مَنَازِلِ الْآخِرَةِ فَإِنْ نَجَا مِنْهُ فَمَا بَعْدَهُ أَيْسَرُ مِنْهُ وَإِنْ لَمْ يَنْجُ مِنْهُ فَمَا بَعْدَهُ أَشَدُّ مِنْهُ

[161] Translator's note: A Sufi mystic and poet who died 632 years after the migration.
[162] Collection of religious verdicts by Ibn Taymiyyah.
[163] Jami' at-Tirmidhī, 2460.

The grave is the first stage of the next world; if one escapes from it what follows is easier than it, but if one does not escape from it what follows is more severe than it.[164]

Stories of the Deceased Who Were Honored After Death

There are numerous narrations mentioning the bliss for the pious within the grave and the punishment for the wicked within the grave, and this is not the place to mention them. Just as Allāh ﷻ might reveal the punishment of some of the deceased to some people from the living, Allāh ﷻ might also reveal forgiveness and honor for some of the deceased to some of the living. This may be witnessed by the living while they are awake, or they might see this in a dream. There are many narrations mentioning this. We will mention some of them, insha'Allāh.

The Story of Daniel

The story of Daniel has been narrated by Abū 'Āliyah.[165] Khalid ibn Dinar said that Abū 'Āliyah said, "When we conquered Shushtar (Iran), we found in the treasury of Hormuzan (the Iranian governor) a bed. Lying on the bed was a deceased man. Sitting next to the man's head was a

[164] *Mishkat al-Masabih*, 132.

[165] Translator's note: He is the noble scholar from the Tābi'īn, Abū 'Āliyah Rufay'a ibn Mihrān. He died 90 years after the migration.

scripture. We took the scripture to 'Umar ibn al-Khattab, and he summoned Ka'b, who translated it into Arabic. I was the first man among the Arabs to read it, and I read it as I read this Qur'ān. I (Khalid) said, 'What was in it?' He said, 'It was about you, your affairs, your religion, your speech, and what will happen after that.' I said, 'What did you do with the man?' He said, 'We dug 13 different graves during the day, then at night we buried him, and we levelled all the graves to conceal its location from the people, so that they would not exhume him.' I said, 'Why would people do that?' He said, 'If rain were withheld from them, they would take his bier out and they would receive rain.' I said, 'Who do you think the man was?' He said, 'A man called Daniel.' I said, 'How long ago do you think he died?' He said, 'Three hundred years ago.' I said, 'Had anything of him changed?' He said, 'No, except a few hairs at the back of his head, for the earth does not consume the bodies of the prophets, and wild animals cannot devour them.'"[166]

Ibn Kathīr said, "This chain of narration is authentic from Abū 'Āliyah, but if the timeline of his death is verified to be 300 years prior to the day they saw him, then he was not a prophet; but rather, he was a righteous man. This is because there was no prophet between Jesus the son of Maryam ﷺ and the Messenger of Allāh ﷺ, based upon a hadīth collected in Sahīh Bukhārī.[167] The time span between Prophet Muhammad and Jesus, peace be upon them, was 400 years. Others say it was 600 years, while some say it was 620 years. The date of his death may have been 800 years prior to the date they saw him, and this is close to the era of Daniel, if it is the same Daniel. Or he could have been another

[166] *Al-Bidāyah wa Nihāyah*, Volume 2, page 40.

[167] Translator's note: The Messenger of Allāh ﷺ said, "I am the nearest of all the people to the son of Mary, and all the prophets are paternal brothers, and there has been no prophet between me and him (Jesus)." Sahīh al-Bukhārī, 3442.

man from the prophets, or a righteous man. But it was most likely Daniel, because Daniel was arrested by the king of the Persians and imprisoned.

Ibn Ishāq, Ibn Jarīr, and others mentioned that Nebuchadnezzar released Daniel from prison after he had a dream and Daniel interpreted it for him. After the dream interpretation, he gave him a garment, walked with him around the village, and gave him a ring. I mentioned his story in my other book about dreams."

THE STORY OF 'ABDULLAH IBN AT-THAMIR

A similar story is the story of 'Abdullāh ibn at-Thāmir. He is the youth mentioned in the long hadīth collected by Ahmad, Muslim, and Tirmidhī from Sahayb ﷺ. In this hadīth, it is mentioned that a king during the era of this youth, killed the youth because he abandoned the religion of the king. After which, all the people embraced the religion of the boy and opposed the religion of the king. Allāh ﷻ mentioned this story in Surah al-Burūj.

﴿ قُتِلَ أَصْحَابُ الْأُخْدُودِ ﴿٤﴾ النَّارِ ذَاتِ الْوَقُودِ ﴿٥﴾ إِذْ هُمْ عَلَيْهَا قُعُودٌ ﴿٦﴾ وَهُمْ عَلَىٰ مَا يَفْعَلُونَ بِالْمُؤْمِنِينَ شُهُودٌ ﴿٧﴾ وَمَا نَقَمُوا مِنْهُمْ إِلَّا أَن يُؤْمِنُوا بِاللَّهِ الْعَزِيزِ الْحَمِيدِ ﴿٨﴾ ﴾

Cursed were the people of the ditch. Fire supplied (abundantly) with fuel, when they sat by it (fire), and they witnessed what they were doing against the believers (burning them). They had nothing against them,

except that they believed in Allāh, the All-Mighty, Worthy of all Praise![168]

A hadīth in *At-Tirmidhī* states, "As for the boy, he was buried." He said, "It has been mentioned that he was excavated during the time of 'Umar bin Al-Khattab, and his finger was at his temple, just as he had placed it when he was killed."[169]

Ibn Ishāq narrated that during the era of 'Umar ibn al-Khattab ﷺ, a man dug up a dilapidated building to retrieve some of his belongings. Upon doing, so he discovered 'Abdullāh ibn at-Thāmir buried beneath the building, sitting with his hand placed over the blow to his head. When his hand was removed, his blood began to flow; when his hand was returned the blood flow stopped. He was wearing a ring. Written on the ring was, 'My Lord is Allāh.' A letter was written to 'Umar ibn al-Khattab informing him of what occurred. 'Umar ﷺ wrote back to them, saying, "Leave him as he is and bury him." And they did as he ordered them to do.

'UMAR IBN AL-KHATTAB AFTER DEATH

From the stories in this category is when the foot of 'Umar ibn al-Khattab appeared. They wanted to expand the Prophet's Masjid during the era of Al-Walīd ibn 'Abdul Mālik, and it had not been previously altered. This was during the 88th year after the migration, 56 years after the death of 'Umar. Ibn Sa'd narrated in the *Tabiqat* from Hishām ibn

168 Sūrah al-Burūj, 85:4-8.

169 Jami' at-Tirmidhī, 3340.

'Urwah, he said, "During the era of Al-Walīd ibn 'Abdul Mālik, they began to expand the masjid of the Prophet ﷺ. While doing so, a wall from the home of the Prophet fell and a foot appeared from a grave. Everyone was alarmed, believing it was the foot of the Prophet ﷺ. No one thought otherwise until 'Urwah[170] said to them, "By Allāh, this is not the foot of the Prophet, it is the foot of 'Umar."

THE BODIES OF THE MARTYRS

Similar stories have been narrated about Hamza ibn 'Abdul Muttalib, 'Abdullāh ibn 'Amr ibn Harām, 'Amr ibn al-Jamūh, and the other martyrs killed at the Battle of Uhud. Their bodies remained fresh, just as the day they were killed. Nothing changed from their bodies many years after they were killed.

Mālik narrated from 'Abdur Rahmān ibn Abī Sa'sa'ah that he had heard that 'Amr ibn al-Jamūh al-Ansārī and 'Abdullāh ibn 'Umar al-Ansārī, both of the tribe of Banū Salami, had their grave uncovered by a flood. Their grave was part of what was left after the flood. They were in the same grave, and they were among those martyred at Uhud. They were dug up so that they might be moved. They were found unchanged. It was as if they had died only the day before. One of them had been wounded, and he had put his hand over his wound and had been buried like that. His hand was pulled away from his wound and released, and it

[170] Translator's note: He is 'Urwah, the son of Zubayr ibn al-Awwam and Asmā bint Abū Bakr. He was from the seven jurists of Madinah, and a leading scholar from the Tābi'īn.

returned to where it had been. There were 46 years between Uhud and the day they were dug up.[171]

Al-Bayhaqī narrated a similar story in *Evidence of Prophecy*, with the following addition. "When Mu'awiyah wanted to repair the cemetery, he had a caller call out to the people of Madinah, 'Whoever has family that were killed at Uhud, let him be present.' So, the people came out to see their deceased family members. Their bodies were wet from the flood, when they wiped their feet, fresh blood began to flow. Abū Sa'īd al-Khudri ﷺ said, 'No one can deny the truth after this.' As they dug the graves, they would take a handful of dirt and the smell of musk would cover them." This was also collected by Ibn Qutaybah in his book *Uyun al-Akhbār*, with an authentic chain of narration.

It was collected by Abū al-Qasim al-Baghawi,[172] with a chain of narration leading to Abū az-Zubayr, that he said, "I heard Jābir ibn 'Abdullāh ﷺ saying, 'When the dam of Uhud sent forth its water, it only flowed into the graves of the martyrs. I saw the people carrying the martyrs on their shoulders, and it appeared as though they were sleeping. The foot of Hamza was accidentally hit, and fresh blood flowed from it.'"

---

[171] *Muwatta Malik,* "Book of Jihād".

[172] Translator's note: He was a scholar of hadīth, and a jurist of Baghdad. He died 317 years after the migration. He was over 100 years old.

Talha ibn 'Ubaydullah

Ibn Abī Dunyā collected the hadīth of Al-Muthana ibn Sa'īd, that he said, "When 'Ā'ishah bint Talha arrived in Basra, a man went to her and said, 'I saw Talha ibn 'Ubaydullah in a dream, and he said to me, 'Tell 'Ā'ishah to move me from this place, because this cold is discomforting.' Therefore, she gathered her guardians and excavated her father. Nothing had changed on his body except for a part of his beard. They then placed him in a new location. There were about 30 years between the time he died and the time his body was moved."

Martyrs from the Battle of al-Yamamah

We were informed by Shaykh 'Abdur Rahmān ibn Fāris ibn 'Abdul 'Azīz al-Fāris, a resident of Riyadh, of the following incident. He said, "A major flood came to the valley of Hanīfah during the year 1359 AH (1940 CE). The flood entered the graves of the companions that were killed during the Battle of al-Yamamah. The Battle of al-Yamamah occurred 11 years after the migration. One of the graves beside the valley was breached such that the body of the deceased was visible outside of the grave." Shaykh 'Abdur Rahmān continued, "When the news reached me, I was in Al-Jubaylah, so I rushed there. The grave had been elevated on the side of the valley such that it could only be reached with a ladder. I grabbed a piece of wood that was supported on the side of grave and climbed it. I saw the deceased and no change at all had occurred to his body. It was as though he was sleeping. He was shrouded in a white cloth which was tied with the leaves from a palm tree. Visible were his face, eyes, teeth, legs, and a lock of his hair. His head was long; thus, it protruded from the grave. I lifted his head, shrouded it, and touched his face with my hand. It was as though I was touching the face of a sleeping man. The complexion of his face was white, inclining toward tan. The hair from his beard was visible and it was neatly combed. His eyes were slightly opened. The palm leaves used to tie his shroud remained green, but it was dry. When the people of the town of Al-Jubaylah heard of him, they came to look at him. The imām of Al-Jubaylah and the president of the Committee for the Promotion of Virtue and the Prevention of Vice went to Shaykh Muhammad Ibrāhīm 'Ālī Shaykh and informed him of this. He ordered him to take some men and place the deceased in a coffin. He told them to dig a grave in the middle of the cemetery during the night and bury him there, and to not inform anyone where he was buried. This was so the people would not be put to trial trying to go to his grave. The men implemented the instructions of Shaykh Muhammad Ibrāhīm."

I say there is no doubt that this deceased man was from the martyrs killed on the battlefield during the war between the Companions and Musaylimah the liar. Therefore, it is assumed that he was from the Companions ﷺ, because it is well-known the cemetery in this place is the cemetery of the Companions. He could also be from those who were not Companions; but rather, fought alongside and assisted the Companions. It is more likely that he was from the Companions, and Allāh ﷻ knows best.

The time span between the Battle of al-Yamamah and the deceased appearing from his grave was 1,348 years. Despite this long timespan, the martyr remained the same without changing at all, even the leaves used to tie his shroud did not change. In this is a lesson for those who have understanding and sound intellect.

SA'D IBN MU'ADH

It was collected by Ibn Sa'd in his *Tabiqat*, narrated from Rabīh ibn 'Abdur Rahmān ibn Abī Sa'īd al-Khudrī that his grandfather said, "I was from those who dug the grave for Sa'd ibn Mu'adh at the cemetery of Al-Baqi. Each time we dug away dirt and the dust arose, we smelled the fragrance of musk until we reached the niche in the grave. Someone took a handful of dirt from his grave and left. When they looked at it later it was musk.

ABU MUHAMMAD AL-BARBAHARI

Ibn al-Jawzī said, "I read from the writing of our Shaykh Abūl Hasan az-Zāguni[173] that he said, 'The grave of Abū Muhammad al-Barbahārī was uncovered, and he was intact. His body had not changed at all. The smell from his grave was that of musk and it filled the city of Bagdad.'"

His statement 'he was intact' means his body was the same then as it was the day he was buried. His name is Abū Muhammad al-Hasan ibn 'Ālī, and he was from the major students of the senior students of Imām Ahmad ibn Hanbal. He has an amazing story that occurred to him after his death, which was a great honor for him. He was stern in rebuking the people of innovation. Consequently, the innovators continued trying to cause the heart of the governor to turn against Al-Barbahārī. The governor gave the order to his chief of police, that he should ride out in public

[173] Translator's note: He is the scholar of his era, Abūl Hasan 'Ālī ibn 'Ubaydullah. He died 527 years after migration.

in Baghdad with the proclamation that no two students of Al-Barbahārī were allowed to meet. Al-Barbahārī was forced to go into hiding.

Muhammad ibn al-Hasan al-Muqri said, "My grandfather, and also my grandmother, related to me that, 'Abū Muhammad al-Barbahārī was hidden by the sister of Tūzūn, in the eastern side of the town, in the alley of the public bathhouse. He was there for about a month, then his blood ceased flowing. When Al-Barbahārī died, still in hiding, the sister of Tūzūn said to her servant, 'Find someone to wash him.' So someone came to wash him and the door was kept locked so that no one would know. He, alone, stood to pray for him, but when the woman who owned the house looked, she found that it was full of men wearing white and green clothing. After he had ended the funeral prayer, she did not see anyone at all, so she called to her servant and said, 'You have destroyed me along with my brother!' So he said, 'Did you not see what I saw?' 'Yes,' she replied. He said, 'Here are the keys to the door and it is still locked.' So she said, 'Bury him in my house; and when I die, bury me near him.'"

A Small Graveyard in Riyadh

We were informed by more than one reliable person that in the city of Riyadh they needed to widen a road known as Al-Wazir Road, from the northern side. To widen the road, they would have to encroach on a part of any old graveyard. They dug up only the graves that desperately needed to be exhumed. They found that all the deceased had become dust, except for one man. This man had not changed at all, except his skin was not soft. He was an elderly man with dyed hair.

Sweet-Scented Plants Inside the Grave

It has been collected by Ibn Abī Dunyā in the book *Tenderness and Crying* that when Al-'Ijli[174] died, they transported him to his grave. When they descended in his grave to guide his body into the niche, they found it filled with sweet-scented plants. Some people took some of the plants and they remained fresh for 70 days without changing. People came from far and near to see the plants. The governor took the plants from the people, fearing it would become a trial for them. He put the plants in his home, and they became lost. He did not know where they went. Ibn Rajab also mentioned this story in his book *Horrors of the Grave.*

The Scent of Perfume from a Dream

From the amazing stories is what has been narrated to us from several reliable men. There was a man named 'Abdul 'Azīz ibn Yahyān from the residents of Riyadh. He was an imām in some of the masājid in Riyadh during the first half of the 14th century, according to the Islāmic calendar. He had memorized the entire Qur'ān and he had a beautiful voice. He had the appearance of righteousness upon him. When 'Abdul 'Azīz died, a man called Hadd as-Sayf saw him in a dream in which he gave him the greeting of salām and hugged him.

Hadd as-Sayf had a practice of going to the masjid during the last part of the night and remaining there until sunrise. Upon leaving the masjid, he would return home and his wife would bring him dates and coffee.

---

[174] Translator's note: He is the scholar of hadīth, Abūl Hasan Ahmad ibn 'Abdullāh ibn Sālih. He died 261 years after migration.

On the morning following the dream in which he saw 'Abdul 'Azīz ibn Yahyān, he returned home. There was a woman in their home who would serve them. This woman smelled a sweet fragrance on him, so she went to his wife and said, "Your husband married another wife last night and the clue of that is the sweet-smelling fragrance coming from him." His wife believed their maid; consequently, she did not bring her husband his dates or coffee that morning as she would normally do. When she did not bring his dates and coffee, he went to her and requested it. She rebuked him and said, "Go to your new wife so she can give you want you want!" He denied having married another wife and swore by Allāh that he did not, but she did not believe him. She said, "This sweet fragrance could only have come from a new wife." He swore a number of times that he did not get married. Then he informed her of what he saw in his dream and that this sweet fragrance attached to him when he shook the hand of 'Abdul 'Azīz ibn Yahyān in his dream.

Those who narrated this story said this fragrance remained with Hadd as-Sayf for a number of days although he performed *wudhu* and washed his hands several times. The smell remained with him for almost one month.

Conclusion

Let the student of knowledge know, the intent for mentioning the stories of punishments in this book is to incite us to take a lesson from what happened to the sinners and to warn against persisting upon sins. Indeed, persisting upon sins is a reason for punishment in this life and has been mentioned in many stories in this book. The fortunate person is the one who learns a lesson from others, and the miserable person is the one who becomes a lesson for others. Allāh ﷻ mentioned the Jews, who violated the Sabbath.

﴿ وَلَقَدْ عَلِمْتُمُ الَّذِينَ اعْتَدَوْا مِنْكُمْ فِي السَّبْتِ فَقُلْنَا لَهُمْ كُونُوا قِرَدَةً خَاسِئِينَ.
فَجَعَلْنَاهَا نَكَالًا لِمَا بَيْنَ يَدَيْهَا وَمَا خَلْفَهَا وَمَوْعِظَةً لِلْمُتَّقِينَ ﴾

And you had already known about those who transgressed among you concerning the Sabbath, and We said to them, 'Be apes, despised.' And We made it a deterrent punishment for those who were present and those who succeeded [them], and a lesson for those who fear Allāh.[175]

Ibn 'Abbās ؓ said, "'A lesson for those who fear Allāh', applies to those who come after them until the Day of Judgment."

Al-Baghawi said, "'A lesson for those who fear Allāh', applies to the believers from the ummah of Muhammad, so they will not commit the same sins the Jews did."

Allāh ﷻ mentioned in His Book the stories of those who opposed the messengers, and the punishment which befell them, to serve as a lesson for the Muslims; and to warn them from the power of Allāh and His revenge. Allāh ﷻ said:

﴿ وَلَا يُرَدُّ بَأْسُنَا عَنِ الْقَوْمِ الْمُجْرِمِينَ ﴾

And Our punishment cannot be repelled from the people who are criminals.[176]

---

[175] Sūrah al-Baqarah, 2:65-66.
[176] Sūrah Yūsuf, 12:110.

Allāh ﷻ said, while warning the wrongdoers from this ummah, lest there should befall them that which befell the people of Lūt from the stones falling upon them:

﴿ فَلَمَّا جَاءَ أَمْرُنَا جَعَلْنَا عَالِيَهَا سَافِلَهَا وَأَمْطَرْنَا عَلَيْهَا حِجَارَةً مِنْ سِجِّيلٍ مَنْضُودٍ. مُسَوَّمَةً عِنْدَ رَبِّكَ وَمَا هِيَ مِنَ الظَّالِمِينَ بِبَعِيدٍ ﴾

So when Our command came, We made the highest part [of the city] its lowest, and rained upon them stones of layered hard clay, [which were] marked from your Lord. And Allāh's punishment is not far from the wrongdoers.[177]

Abū Bakr al-Hudhali said, concerning the statement of Allāh ﷻ, "And Allāh's punishment is not far from the wrongdoers," [that] the punishment is not far from the wrongdoers of this ummah. Therefore, no criminal should feel safe from it.

Therefore, fear Allāh, those who oppose the command of Allāh ﷻ and the command of His Messenger ﷺ. Do not minimize opposing the commands and partaking in the prohibitions. Do not persist upon sins lest you be afflicted with the same punishment that befell those who persisted upon sins before you. The Prophet ﷺ said:

وَيْلٌ لِلْمُصِرِّينَ الَّذِينَ يُصِرُّونَ عَلَى مَا فَعَلُوا وَهُمْ يَعْلَمُونَ

Woe to those who persist (upon sins), those who consciously persist upon what they are doing while they know.[178]

---

177 Sūrah Hūd, 11:82-83.

178 Al-Adab al-Mufrad, 380.

Allāh ﷻ is the One we ask to grant me and all the Muslims success in actions He is pleased with and to protect us from being exposed to His wrath and anger. Indeed, Allāh is the Guardian for this, and He has the ability to do so. May Allāh ﷻ raise the rank and send peace upon our Prophet Muhammad and upon his family, his Companions and those who follow them in goodness upon the Day of Judgment.

The completion of writing this treatise occurred on Thursday, corresponding to the 11th day of the month of Muharram, in the year 1411 after the Hijrah, by the hand of the one in absolute need of Allāh ﷻ, Hamūd ibn 'Abdullāh al-Tuwaijri. May Allāh ﷻ forgive him, his parents, and the believing men and the believing women. And all praises belong to Allāh, the One Who by way of His virtue the good deeds are completed.